CLICK

Sarah,
Thanks for your support on this journey. I truly appreciate everything you do for me.

.

Click

**Transform Your Business
Through Digital Marketing**

Kevin Wilhelm

LIONCREST
PUBLISHING

CLICK

Transform Your Business Through Digital Marketing

ISBN   978-1-5445-0525-1 *Hardcover*

       978-1-5445-0523-7 *Paperback*

       978-1-5445-0524-4 *Ebook*

I would like to dedicate this book to every entrepreneur or business owner who is giving it their all to make tomorrow better than today. You're the ones who go out each and every day and grind, hustle, and leave it all out on the field. I hope this book provides you some level of support on your journey.

Contents

Introduction

DIGITAL MARKETING: MORE THAN NICE TO HAVE

Imagine growing your revenue by over $10 million per year.

That's the story of Action Furnace, a local furnace company, who, in a five-year span, and as a thirty-five-year-old business, grew from $9 million to over $20 million in annual sales.

Think about that:

It took them *thirty years* to reach $9 million in sales, then it took just *five years* to get to over $20 million in sales.

Was it because they fundamentally changed their business strategy? Did they offer different products or lower prices? No.

They did it in large part by approaching their digital marketing differently—*strategically*.

Bruce, the owner of Action Furnace, was spending about $20,000 a month on marketing. To most small-to medium-sized businesses, that amount seems absurd, but he'd grown that investment over the past decade, slowly adding more investment as his business grew.

He *thought* he had outsourced his digital marketing effectively, but because he wasn't using a cohesive strategy, he was still having to make all the decisions himself, coming up with all the ideas, and managing multiple marketing projects. But Bruce's expertise is in his business, not in marketing.

Despite his significant time and financial investments, the phone didn't ring as often as he wanted it to, and he was frustrated by numerous inefficient marketing meetings. He knew that improvements could be made—he knew there must be a better way.

When Bruce and I met, he was at his breaking point—frustrated because he knew there was a better way to approach his marketing, a more efficient way to grow his business. We developed a detailed marketing plan (the same kind I'll help you develop in this book), which gave us a specific direction to craft a new strategy and determine new, realistic, and effective digital marketing budgets. The plan was a significant departure from what he was currently doing—what had made him so successful up to this point. We're talking a complete overhaul to his website, Google Ads strategy, SEO strategy, and implementing digital display advertising for the first time...not to mention an introduction to YouTube marketing when few small businesses were investing in it at the time.

At first, Bruce resisted all the suggested changes in front of him (don't we all?). The risk of the unknown made him uneasy, and he felt he had a lot to lose. He had built a successful business, and he wondered if the frustrations he felt over his marketing were really big enough to justify a change in direction.

So what finally convinced Bruce to make the change? He realized that if he didn't make a move to increase his company's position in the market, he would continue down the same path he had been on for years—with less growth than he'd hoped for.

The details of the changes we made aren't important at

this point—you'll learn the methods to make your own in this book—but the gist of it was this: with a different approach and viewpoint for his marketing, he was able to build a profitable marketing engine that brought him reliable, predictable, and sustainable leads to his business—day after day, year after year. And now, his business has doubled in under five years with no sign of slowing down.

MUST-HAVES

If you're a business owner who believes your products, services, and operations are already in decent shape, you might just need more people to know about you. If you already have a framework in place to allow for exponential growth in your business, you just have to find more prospective customers, wherever they may be hiding.

Exponential growth is absolutely possible for any business willing to learn, adopt, and follow the actions laid out in this book.

If you're similar to Bruce at Action Furnace, then you know there's a better way to be doing digital marketing, but you don't know what that is yet. You might have built a website two years ago and haven't touched it since. You might invest little to nothing in marketing and advertising and instead focus on the operations of your business. You might not have time to stay on top of the changing behavior of your consumers, or their changing use of technology. You're probably not sure how much to spend, where to spend it, and where to cut back when it's not working.

It can be hard sometimes to trust vendors or marketers because many use fear tactics—*if you don't advertise exactly the same way we tell you to, you'll go out of business*—but you're worried that if you spend *too much money* on it, you'll be left with nothing anyway.

So you might be sitting here feeling paralyzed. When left powerless, you might wind up making a token effort to market yourself better or avoid it altogether.

Even if you're the rare breed that does understand marketing to a certain extent, it's likely rarer still that you have time to do it properly, because marketing always seems like a nice-to-have, not a must-have.

Collecting accounts receivables is a *must-have*.

Submitting payroll is a *must-have*.

Producing your product or delivering on your service is a *must-have*.

Marketing? That's nice to have...right?

Not in my book.

WIIFY: WHAT'S IN IT FOR YOU?

This book is written for you, the business owner who doesn't know where to start. By the time you finish reading this book, you will have tangible, concrete, actionable steps to improve your digital marketing. It's easy to read, digestible, specific, and I'll give you an action plan to implement it. I'll help you figure out how much to spend, where to spend it, and how to know when it's working.

So who the hell am I to tell you all this stuff?

I was born in the digital age, but I wasn't born into digital marketing. In fact, I was born into a sales family of all things. My parents are lifetime salespeople with an overwhelming natural ability to make anyone buy anything from them. My family also bought and operated a local restaurant and lounge after I graduated from high school. I worked there while I was in university, so I understand both small business and family business. I understand the sacrifices required to make it all work. I understand what it's like to not take a paycheck for three years (thanks, Mom and Dad). I understand the importance of paying your employees first, even if that comes at the cost of paying yourself less...or not at all.

When I went to university at the University of Calgary, I knew I wanted to major in business commerce, but I was two years in before I knew what I wanted to specialize in. Then I attended my first marketing course. Immediately after I left my first class, I assigned myself as a marketing major—and I've never looked back. I started my career working for the Yellow Pages, helping business owners find digital and print marketing solutions for their businesses. From that experience, I spoke to hundreds of business owners about their challenges, struggles, and opportunities they just couldn't make time for and their perception of how often marketing fit into their day-to-day operations (somewhere between never and almost never).

I left after a couple of years to head up the marketing department for a national childcare company called BrightPath, where I learned the inner workings of the corporate world. I went from *selling* ad space to *buying* it, learning what it was like to be on *your* side of the negotiating table as an entrepreneur, as a marketer.

I then left at the beginning of 2014 to create my own agency—a place where we could truly partner with businesses, implement my marketing strategies, and help businesses grow *profitably*. My partners and I created a vision where we built a network of marketing agencies that all specialized in specific industries. To date, we employ over thirty marketing experts and have worked with well over a hundred entrepreneur-led businesses—helping them all seize the opportunity in front of them.

A DIGITAL MARKETER BY YOUR SIDE

Think of this book like having a digital marketer by your side through every step of the process.

Having said that, this is *not* a topical book with current statistics. The strategies you read here were relevant five years ago, and they'll continue to be relevant five years from tomorrow.

Likewise, the advice in this book is not for the big brands of the world. It's for you: the entrepreneur-led business that is motivated to grow—quickly, efficiently, and profitably. Working with large companies doesn't excite me like it does for most marketers; we started our agency because we truly wanted to help people *like you*. By reading this book, I now consider you to be one of my clients. So expect me to treat you like any other client I care about. Because I do.

Are you ready for exponential growth? Let's go.

Part 1

Digital Marketing Basics

—

CHAPTER 1

Creating a Marketing Plan

If you're like the majority of business owners, you live day to day, decision to decision. While you worry about today, tomorrow, and next month, you lose yourself in the details.

So when you consider creating something as abstract and as seemingly inconsequential as a marketing plan? Ha! Why bother?

You make hundreds of decisions on a daily basis, ranging from creating invoices to handling unpaid bills, to hiring, to fulfilling orders. Until someone walks a mile in your shoes, they wouldn't even *begin* to realize the thousands of concerns that pass through your head as an entrepreneur.

You work *hard* in your business.

But there's a big difference between working *on* your business and working *in* your business. Most owners are so trapped on working in the day-to-day that they rarely take a step back to see their business from a 10,000-foot level. As a result, they lose the big picture.

In this chapter, I'll teach you how to develop a marketing plan that takes into account the near, distant, and profitable future.

FOCUS ON YOUR "MUST-HAVES"

You know, it's funny: a marketing plan is actually a tactical, day to day part of your business—despite what I said just a few paragraphs ago—but its strategy comes from an abstract vision for your company's future.

What will your industry look like in ten years?

Who are your customers today?

Who do you want your customers to be in ten years?

How are those customers' habits changing?

Those are the questions you should answer in your marketing plan.

Most marketing decisions are made by victims of the moment. You can't make an effective marketing plan based on what happened to you this morning. For example, you might look at your quarterly financials at the end of a bad quarter. Naturally, you decide to cut into your marketing budget because you think that'll help free up cash flow. Then, down the line, you experience another bad quarter as a result of acquiring fewer customers. Did that initial cost-cutting move help your business in the long term, or did it just make you *feel better* about your business in the moment you made the decision?

Soon enough, if you continue to make huge changes based on short-term fears, you find yourself stuck on a path where you make moves without rhyme or reason. A path without clear objectives, one that doesn't involve consideration for your customers or their budgets, is ultimately not rooted in reality. Whenever a new competitor enters the market, you feel threatened. You put pressure on yourself to market better, but you don't know how—digital marketing changes so quickly that you don't even know where to start...

WHAT ARE THE BENEFITS OF
DIGITAL MARKETING?

Digital marketing exists to tell your brand's story to an audience through digital media, such as Google Ads and YouTube.

More old-fashioned forms of "interactions," like TV, radio, and newspaper, are often referred to as traditional marketing.

Consumers have completely changed how they consume media. People interact with brands, companies, and ideas in totally new ways—such as social media, videos, and branded entertainment—because we live online. As such, digital marketing is the widest avenue to reach audiences.

Now, where do I even begin with the benefits of digital marketing?

Not only does digital marketing have a wide reach, it can also be targeted toward specific customers. For example, imagine a prospective customer calls your company about a product or service. As a business owner, you can see exactly what that customer did on your website and how long they spent there. You can see whether they visited your LinkedIn page, read your blogs, and watched your videos.

Through digital marketing, all of this information becomes available to you instantly. Your responsibility as a business owner is to use this information to make better decisions for your business on a go-forward basis.

And the best part? All of the processes in digital marketing can be automated, and they can be done relatively inexpensively. As a business owner, you can distribute your messaging digitally at a fraction of what traditional media would cost you (because you don't have to pay for postage or shipping).

THE FIRST STEP

The first step to creating a marketing plan is to understand where you are today. If you don't know where you are, you can't know where you're going.

Take a piece of paper and write down the following:

1. Your financial figures for your last fiscal year (as in your current revenue and gross profit margin).
2. Your current customers (How old are they? Where do they live? What do they want?).
3. The avenues through which you reach those customers currently.
4. How much it costs to reach those customers.

REMEMBER THE RISK

Imagine your company is currently selling primarily to baby boomers. When those customers age, they might not need your product anymore. In that case, how are you going to replace the lost revenue from that product in five years if your primary customer base no longer buys it?

One strategy might be to create a product that appeals to a younger demographic. However, if you change all of your marketing to attract younger people, you might alienate your current demographic, which makes up, say, 85 percent of your revenue. While that marketing strategy might work ten years down the line, it could be detrimental in the short term, because you're neglecting your current customers.

If you find yourself in this position, you need a transition plan.

LOWERING LEVI'S AVERAGE AGE

Let's examine Levi's jeans. From 1996 to 2001, the iconic clothing company saw revenue drop from $7.1 billion in sales to $4.1 billion. They lost almost half of their business. Young shoppers were choosing younger brands, and the company was in disarray.

In 2011, Levi's hired a new CEO (Chip Bergh), and he implemented a new strategy to rejuvenate the brand. Initially, they only focused on their profitable sectors—Levi's men's bottoms and Dockers's men's bottoms—while eliminating the areas that were draining resources. This freed up available cash to concentrate on new and promising areas of the business. They wanted to concentrate on a younger demographic with products that had high potential and were underserved.

Today, Levi's offers stretch wear, women's wear, and has partnered with Google to have a smart shirt that allows you to control your clothes with your phone. What have the results been? Over the past seven years, the average age of a Levi's consumer has decreased from forty-seven to thirty-four. Sales are up and continue to be on the rise.

Changing a marketing strategy is always risky, especially when it could alienate your current customer base. But the potential reward might be massive.

MARKETING VS. SALES

As a business owner, it's important to get a clear picture of how much you spend on marketing.

> Remember: marketing includes everything from putting up a poster in a store, to sending an email, to your voicemail greeting.

Now, most small business owners mess this up, but it's true: there's a difference between sales and marketing. Strong sales do not necessarily equate to strong marketing, and vice versa. For example, you might have an ineffective marketing strategy, but your business continues to grow because you have one great salesperson. Your entire business is essentially leveraged behind that one employee. If that salesperson were to leave, your business would find itself in a very precarious position. You have operated under the illusion that your marketing strategy is great, but really, it was a great salesperson who has helped plug the gap.

> The better your marketing is, the less competent and talented your salespeople actually have to be.

One of the hardest challenges for any business is to build a happy customer base. However, if your marketing is amazing and customers want your product, *they* will call *you*. If that happens, all a salesperson has to do is not mess up the sale.

However, if you haven't created a solid marketing plan, your salespeople are calling *them* about a product they haven't heard of. In that instance, your sales team has to be incredibly convincing.

While many business owners are quick to cut marketing, they fail to realize that investing in marketing can save them a lot of money on their business development costs. If you feed leads to your salespeople or make the sales cycle shorter, their commission doesn't need to be as high.

A good marketing plan will elevate a mediocre sales team to an excellent one. Alternatively, a lack of marketing can reduce the effectiveness of a great sales team down to mediocrity.

PICTURE SUCCESS

Your next step in developing your marketing plan is to ask yourself, "What does success look like three years from today? Where do I want to be?"

To continue with your marketing plan, complete the following statements:

- Three years from today, our revenue will be _____.
- Three years from today, our profit will be _____.
- Three years from today, our gross profit percentage will be _____.

- Three years from today, our customers will be made up of _____.

Regarding that final question: Will your customers shift generations (such as shifting your focus from baby boomers to millennials)? What will that shift look like?

Once you have completed this exercise, ask yourself the same questions for a year from now. This might seem backward—to start with three years in the future, *then* move to one year in the future—but it works better for one reason: to ensure that you are on track to achieve your three-year plan, you have to ask yourself where you have to be a year from today.

LES'S NOT TUBS

Les Svindt is the owner of Patioline and is in the patio furniture and hot tub business. His hot tubs account for 15 percent of his revenue. However, they also account for 40 percent of his *marketing*. This isn't just a poor investment; it also creates a confusing brand message. So he decides to get rid of hot tubs altogether. By doing so, he knows he's sacrificing some of his revenue, but he also frees up his marketing budget and cleans up his message.

By giving up on hot tubs, he becomes even more specialized and sees an increase in sales. This is a perfect example of how marketing and business come together to increase revenue.

BREAK DOWN YOUR GOALS

As you break down your goals, think about them through two lenses: lead generation and advertising/branding. Although they might seem similar, these concepts are totally different.

- Lead generation is all about acquiring the next customer *today* as profitably as you can.
- Advertising/branding means creating a brand name in your market with your products for your customers of *tomorrow*.

LEAD GENERATION

Successful lead generation requires capturing the current demand in the market for your product. Right now, in your city, there are people looking online for what you have to offer. Are they going to come to you or your competitors? Your job is to make sure that you show up on Google search results first, so they come to you, and not the guy on the other side of town.

Once your customers do find your business, you need to present compelling reasons *why* customers should do business with you. Then you need to make the online experience as easy as possible to get the prospect into the sales funnel.

Think of lead generation as showing up for the people already looking for your product. As a business, you're capturing their demand, handing them off to the next step in the sales process, and making it easy for them to do business with you.

Lead generation requires a competitive mentality. You need to show up for all stages of a customer's buying cycle. This means understanding where customers are looking for your products. For example, they might use review sites or directories. They might be on social media, asking their friends, or doing Google searches. As a business, you should be in those same places to control the story of your product. To do this, you need the necessary fuel. This means having the right marketing plan in place to allot time to these ventures. Without a plan, you'll struggle to show up when a potential customer searches for you.

ADVERTISING AND BRANDING

As a business owner, you won't always interact with a prospect who needs your product today. Instead, you're speaking to everyone who might need your product tomorrow, next month, or next year. By talking to your future customers today, you create trust, familiarity, and a sense of emotional connection between a problem and how your product can solve it. That way, when customers are presented with that problem in the future, they instantly think about your product as the solution.

SLEEP COUNTRY CANADA

On average, there are about two weeks between the moment you decide to buy a mattress and the moment you actually make the purchase. In those two weeks, you might visit three mattress stores, get quotes from each, and try various mattresses for comfort.

Sleep Country Canada is one of the biggest Canadian mattress companies. Their marketing goal is simple: to be one of those three stores that you visit in your mattress-buying process. In that sense, they are successful. I challenge you to find a Canadian who would not list Sleep Country as one of their top three mattress brand retailers.

Notice: *you don't have to be the first company they think of (although that would be nice), but you do need to be in the top three in order to be considered as a contender. Most people will include three options in their buying decision.*

Imagine you're craving a fast food hamburger. Are you going to hop on Google and type in "fast food hamburger near me"? Hell no! You can list the fast food chains off the top of your head. And odds are, one of those chains will be McDonald's.

Over the years, McDonald's has spent *billions* of dollars to create that primacy in your mind—to make sure that when I say fast food hamburger, you immediately think of McDonald's.

That's the point of advertising, branding, and your overall marketing plan: to be top of mind for your service within your city, state, or province.

> If you are a newer or less established business, the majority (if not all) of your budget should be put toward lead generation to start. Chances are you're in survival mode. You need customers to buy your products, use your products, and then spread the word about your brand—fast.

ACTION FURNACE

When you feel like you want to pull back on marketing, my suggestion is simple:

Don't.

Instead, change *the way* you market. Utilize your big reach. Put the majority of your budget toward digital advertising and branding. Focus on your client of the future. Protect your market share even if you aren't interested in growing it.

Action Furnace originally grew exclusively through lead generation efforts—they invested a lot of money, but that investment yielded them significant results. Whenever someone searched *furnace* or *furnace repair in Calgary,* Action Furnace showed up at the top. Soon enough, the company wasn't able to grow at the same rate anymore using the same tactics. Their growth rate had slowed simply because they were maxing out the opportunity of reaching all the people on search engines looking for their products and services. In other words, they were showing up all the time for every search relevant to their business. We had to think beyond the search engine to continue to foster their growth. At that point, the company needed to convince people who *hadn't* already been thinking about furnaces to start thinking about them. That's where the advertising kicked in.

To create an effective marketing plan, the leadership at Action Furnace needed to decide who their most valuable customers were. We worked with Bruce, the owner, to change the course of his company for the better:

We created a persona for his target customer and did so by answering the following questions (and more):

- What does my target customer do for a living?
- Which route do they drive to work?
- Do they live downtown or in the suburbs?
- What radio stations do they listen to?
- What videos do they watch on YouTube?
- Which websites did they spend time on?
- Why do they need a new furnace?

Together, we then created advertising messaging to solve

that persona's furnace problems. Through that process, Action Furnace decided to implement a new slogan: *Fixed Right or It's Free*. After much discussion, it was decided that the slogan was catchy and spoke directly to their customers' pain points. When someone has a broken furnace, all they want is a guarantee that it can be fixed.

This messaging was broadcast to the whole city, and it started to work. The brand recall of Action Furnace has increased dramatically, and they have become one of, if not the most, sought-after furnace repair company in the city.

Over time, Bruce noticed that the number of people who searched for his website *directly* increased significantly. People weren't just looking for any furnace repair company; they searched for Action Furnace specifically.

> Notice that our messaging specifically included the idea of fixing. Most people don't think to buy a new furnace until theirs stops working. Therefore, Action Furnace focuses on furnace fixes and are able to recommend a new furnace when it's warranted.
>
> It's important to note that Action Furnace doesn't and will never offer the *cheapest* furnace repairs. For that reason, we didn't want their slogan to promote them being low cost. That would be misleading. Instead, they wanted a slogan to characterize them as a quick and reliable company with a high competence level.

As soon as Action Furnace developed their marketing plan, they had more traffic coming into their website.

Over the last five years, they have achieved exponential growth. For a local service company like Action Furnace, going from $9 million to over $20 million in five years is phenomenal growth, and evidence of effective marketing and operations.

DEVELOPING *YOUR* MARKETING PLAN

Every business owner should understand the repercussions of their strategies. When you launch a lead generation strategy, you might be able to generate some leads instantly. And when you launch an advertising strategy, it might take months to actually see results and have customers reach out to your business.

But when you integrate both lead generation and advertising/branding in a cohesive and targeted marketing plan, you *click* with the customers you want to attract.

Now that you know who you want to work with and where you want to go, let's give you enough gas to get there. Let's talk budgeting.

CHAPTER 2

How to (Re)Invest in Marketing

Imagine you're walking down the street and you see a machine with a sign on it. As you get closer, you can finally make out what the sign says:

DIGITAL MARKETING

Insert $1 and get $10 back!

If you're like most people, you're skeptical, to say the least. But you have a dollar in your pocket. What else would you use that dollar for—you can't even buy a coffee with a buck. Are you going to take the risk? What if you do insert your dollar and actually get $10 in return?

Then what?

Most entrepreneurs seem too afraid to put that first dollar in—which seems odd to me because, by definition, an entrepreneur is someone willing to take a risk to make a profit. So, they're either afraid to invest their first dollar, or put the first dollar in and run away without seeing whether the machine spit out any money in return.

As an entrepreneur, you need a plan (look back to your answers from the last chapter). However, having a plan is not enough. You need to *believe* that your plan will work, and be willing to invest the money into digital marketing and have enough dedication and focus to wait for the $10 to come out.

My goal is to convince you that such a machine *does* exist, and it's safe for you to put your dollar(s) in. Trust me—the $10 will come out. And here's the crazier part: putting that dollar in the machine isn't a gamble. Hell, it's not even an expense.

It is an *investment* with an expected return. A profitable return.

AN INVESTABLE EXPENSE

Many business owners make the mistake of assigning marketing as an expense line in their business. An investment is different. In business, an investment is a cost with an expectation of return.

Consider marketing as an investable expense. Articulate this expectation. Write it down. Share it with your team. That way, everybody knows the rules of the game your business is playing. If you don't share your expectation, you risk not understanding your true return on investment. In that case, how can you know whether your investment is working?

If you have a plan but don't share it with anybody, you can't expect everyone to be aligned with your vision. I encourage you to be open. Share your growth projections with your employees. Be open about your marketing budget and expected return. Share these figures with your vendors, employees, and partners. Make sure everyone knows the rules of the game you're playing.

For example, every retail store should want a pleasant retail environment. In that case, you might invest in halogen lights for your jewelry store to help sell more diamond necklaces and engagement rings. Good lighting in a fitting room will also help increase sales. Victoria's Secret use scent in their stores to create a better shopping experience, brand loyalty, and higher purchase points.

The point is, no business would ever spend money on lighting, scents, or training without the expectation that the *investment* would drive revenue or increase costs elsewhere in the company.

Similarly, why would you expect a return on investment if you haven't made an investment in the first place?

FILL YOUR TANK WITH FUEL

Let's use cars as an analogy for your marketing. Simply putting a flyer into your local newspaper would be the equivalent of driving a compact car. Or you can build an extremely robust marketing strategy, which means you're now driving a high-performance sports car. The high-performance sports car and a compact car will both get you to your destination, but the sports car is going to get you there more quickly and efficiently.

Sticking with this analogy, if digital marketing is the vehicle that will get your business to the revenue and profit you want to reach, think of your budget as the gas. No matter how beautiful your vehicle (or no matter how well conceived your marketing plan), you will never reach your destination if your car doesn't have enough gas.

Most business owners are too quick to cut marketing budgets. Either that, or they never give their plans enough fuel to begin with. And yet they still expect to get to their destination!

When a marketing plan runs out of fuel before it gets to the finish line, this ruins morale in the office. Employees lose confidence in you as an owner.

Imagine: things get bad in your company for a few months—you hit a dip in sales. If you cut marketing, you're essentially choosing to run out of gas. You're choosing not to reach your destination. You're choosing not to compete.

Some business owners are quick to blame everything and everyone but themselves. For example, if they don't reach a goal, they might blame the economy, their staff, or market changes. In reality, the business didn't reach its growth goal because it wasn't provided enough fuel to get there.

If you want to grow your business by 30 percent, but you only invest 2 percent of your budget to digital marketing, what do you think will happen?

Or looking at it another way: if you want to drive 300 miles, but you only put two gallons of gas in your tank, how far do you think you'll go?

I want you to imagine you are running a large childcare company. You have 100 open spaces, and you would love to fill them all. You know the average cost per acquisition of a new client (child) is $200. To fill those 100 spaces, you will need a pretty healthy marketing budget (100 spaces x $200 target cost per acquisition = $20,000...at least). But currently, you only have a budget of $8,000 in marketing.

While that number seems high, that's too small.

Divide your $8,000 budget by your $200 target cost-per-acquisition fee, and it's easy to see that, if successful, you will fill forty spaces. While forty spaces is still considered a successful result, you weren't able to reach your larger goal of filling all available spaces because your marketing was underfunded. While you ran a profitable campaign, you didn't have enough fuel to get yourself across the finish line.

THE FORMULA

Back to your current reality. Based on your capacity today, what is the maximum number of consumers you could service?

Compare how many you have today to how many you want to serve tomorrow.

If you're a real estate broker, think about how many deals you can handle before you're unable to offer quality service. If you run a restaurant, how many tables do you have available before you have to start turning people away?

To optimize your capacity through lead generation, you have to understand what your average customer is worth to your business. Let's say your average product sells for $1,000. What is your commission payout on a $1,000 sale? Are you willing to pay the same rate on a referral fee?

In any industry, you should think about your capacity for new business. Take your cost-per-acquisition target and multiply it by your remaining capacity. That's one way to help you determine your marketing budget.

Target cost per acquisition x your remaining capacity = your ideal marketing budget

You can always work backward if you prefer. For example, you have twenty-five available spots and each client is worth $1,000. If you fill all the spots, you'll have $25,000 in revenue. Ask yourself how much you'd be willing to invest to get $25,000 in revenue.

HIGH- AND LOW-MARGIN BUSINESS

If you run a high-margin business, you should be willing to invest more.

I have a friend who owns a boutique fitness space and their gross margins are more than 70 percent! They can afford to invest more in marketing because it doesn't cost much to service each customer—they already have the space, they already have the equipment, and they already have the employees. It's just a matter of getting more butts through the door.

If you have a low-margin business—where you have to pay more money per customer—you may not be able to invest as much in marketing. Either way, don't spitball it. Look at your numbers.

THE YELLOW PAGES MENTALITY

For 120 years, small business owners relied on the Yellow Pages for their marketing. They could purchase a quarter-, half-, or full-page ad, and that would be enough to generate business for an entire year.

Those were the days...

The problem was that their marketing investment would only generate as much interest as the Yellow Pages itself. Here's what I mean: your ad could only reach as many people as the book reached. And once your ad printed, you were locked in at that price and size. You weren't able to adjust your advertising investment for the rest of the year—whether you wanted to decrease it if it wasn't working or increase it if it was.

Moreover, you'd have no idea what your competitors were doing that same year (until the book actually came out), and you had little insight into whether your customers came from your Yellow Pages ad or another form of marketing. It was a shot in the dark.

People made an important business decision based on the distribution of a hundred-year-old book. To a certain extent, that mindset still exists today.

But it doesn't have to. With digital marketing today, we're free of the shackles and limitations of print-based marketing. Regardless of what type of ad you run, you can track, change, and adjust everything in real time.

Are you guilty of the Yellow Pages mentality of getting locked into a single narrow form of marketing and not changing? Maybe. Are your competitors? Likely. Either way, you have an opportunity ahead of you...

WHAT SHOULD YOU DO INSTEAD?

How exactly does the Yellow Pages mentality manifest today?

Some digital marketing agencies ask you to lock in for long periods of time without your knowing whether their "magic" is working or not.

You should choose marketing partners who don't have restrictive contracts, and don't hold you to crazy fees. Invest as much as you want—based on actual calculations—and increase your investment in what works and decrease what doesn't work.

> The final chapters of this book will provide you with all the tools you need to enact a digital marketing plan for yourself. You'll also receive guidance about whether you should build your own digital marketing plan, or whether you should hire out marketers to make one for you.

THE $50,000-A-MONTH BUDGET

I listened to Bruce's sales calls early in the process with Action Furnace. After doing so, we determined the close rate and the average cost per sale. From there, we put a marketing budget in place to see how many more service calls their repair technicians could make per month. We then calculated how many of those service calls led to a furnace replacement, as opposed to a furnace repair.

Based on those numbers, we calculated Bruce's marketing budget. At first, it seemed big and scary: nearly $50,000 per month. While this was a lot more money than he'd ever spent, the figures made sense. In order to maximize his schedule, Bruce would have to spend $50,000 per month. Without that investment, he wouldn't fill his schedule or achieve his target revenue. Without a full schedule, his staff sat idle and contemplated leaving for another opportunity.

Luckily, he believed in the marketing plan we had built. He agreed to implement the marketing campaign. What happened? We saw results almost immediately. Action Furnace's phone rang more than it ever had before, and Bruce's schedule filled up at lightning speed.

In the world of digital marketing, if you decide to use $50,000 to market your business, you don't need to spend $50,000 today. When businesses relied on the Yellow Pages for advertising, they *were* expected to spend all of their marketing budget at once. A company would write a check, wait for the book, and see their ad. From there, anything could happen.

With digital marketing, you can pay per click. Channels like Google, YouTube, Instagram, and Facebook are tied to your credit card, and you are only charged when someone clicks on your ad. In theory, your return should be almost immediate. As time goes on, you might learn that it takes five people to click on an ad to call you. In one day, you might spend $50 in clicks, but you also generate a new sale worth $1,000. Before you even make your credit card payment for your Google campaign, you've billed and received money from your customer.

The moral of this story is that you have to be willing to invest money in digital marketing to grow your business. This is how Action Furnace became so successful. As time went on, we evaluated the strategy and increased their budget according to their capacity. When Bruce's schedule became totally full and there was no more available labor, we paused the advertising.

THE IMPORTANCE OF BRUCE

Through his research and entrepreneurial experience, Bruce knew that a person would get three quotes from companies before buying a new furnace, meaning that his company had a 33 percent chance to win that customer. But that wasn't good enough for Bruce. He wanted to increase his odds.

Now, Google has a rule that a company cannot compete with itself online. In other words, there can't be two Action Furnace ads fighting against each other.

Bruce knew how effective online advertising could be. We created a competing company to market against him. Together, we created a second furnace company with different trucks, different clothing, and different invoicing. Through this second company, Bruce entered the market selling the same product under a different brand. We even created a new website and competed head to head.

Bruce was willing to invest in a competing business, which was called Furnace Doctor. He knew that if he could increase the number of quotes he gave, everything else in the business would line up.

If that doesn't show a belief in marketing, I don't know what does.

Here's a business owner who paid to compete against himself for clicks. Clearly, Bruce understands the importance of marketing as a competitive advantage. By being so dialed into the numbers, Bruce doesn't become irresponsible with marketing. Although his budget is probably higher than most of his competitors, his risk is lower. Bruce knows where every single dollar goes and the return he gets for it.

While one business owner might spend $1,000 on marketing without knowing whether or not the strategy is working, Bruce can spend $100,000 on marketing and know his ROI to the penny. He knows his numbers better than any client I have ever worked with.

RESPONSIBLE RISKS

To quote the great Bruce Arians, "No risk-it, no biscuit." It takes money to make money. Unfortunately, there's no way around that. To increase revenue, you have to take risks. Think of business like the stock market: you have to invest in stocks in order to make money off them. Putting money into your marketing budget is like investing in a company you know the best: your own.

Nobody expects you to back up a Brinks truck to the Digital Marketing machine and load in 50,000 $1 bills (we call those Loonies in Canada) from day one. Even if that $50,000 were successful, you have to carefully consider whether your operations could handle that many increased leads. For example, imagine your phone rings forty times a day. Do you have the manpower within the company to handle these calls?

I encourage you to keep your investments comfortable, especially in the first month and first quarter. Have tracking in place to review how effective the investment is over time. When you see a strategy is working, you can put more money into it. The more you reinvest, the more you can move toward your goal.

That's what makes digital marketing a magic machine for your business.

LEARN WHEN TO CUT

Don't be afraid to make cuts in areas that aren't working. There's a fine line between having patience for a process and desperately holding on when you shouldn't (that's when you have to decide whether to reinvest). I see a lot of people holding on to processes that worked in the past. Just because an investment worked at one point doesn't mean it'll continue to work forever. Personally, I struggle to understand why people still invest in the Yellow Pages or newspapers. Old habits are difficult to break.

As soon as you realize that a better option exists, you become more confident about moving forward.

When it comes to your business, look closely at the numbers and the associated ROI. Give tactics enough time, but stop funneling money toward those that clearly aren't working. As part of the marketing plan, you'll create quarterly objectives. Whenever you launch a strategy, you can analyze it at every quarter. If the strategy doesn't become profitable in two or three quarters, it's time to try something else.

While it's important to research, develop, and test tactics, it's equally as important to recognize when an approach doesn't work and move on to the next.

CHAPTER 3

———

SEO Basics

Let's begin this chapter with a game of dares.

I'll start. I dare you to hop onto Google and type your city followed by your service or industry.

Calgary Furnace Repair.

Albany Auto Mechanic.

Seattle Dentist.

Do you show up first or tenth? Are you even on the first page, or are you so deep into the Google results that you might as well be invisible?

The companies that show up before you—your competitors *in your city*—don't own that real estate by accident (and if they do, they'll be even easier for you to overtake).

They've risen through the search rankings by practicing search engine optimization (or SEO, as you've possibly heard it).

As a business owner, you may be getting pitched by SEO managers as often as three times a week. My guess is that you've had one of three experiences with SEO. You've either:

- Never heard of it, or
- Never invested in it, or
- You have invested in it, but you were burned by someone who didn't get results.

In this chapter, I'm going to give you the basics of SEO so you know why it's important to invest in it, how to engage in meaningful conversation, *and* how to hold your SEO manager accountable to their plan and results.

GETTING IN TOUCH WITH SEO

SEO can sound nebulous and abstract, but in simple terms it just refers to the work necessary for a business to show up organically whenever someone searches for their service. That's it. However, your difficulty comes from not knowing *how* to show up organically on search results.

> Every business owner knows they should show up higher in Google. That's a fact. But unless you have some idea of how that happens, you'll pay an SEO "expert" without asking the important questions, for fear of looking out of touch.
>
> From that insecurity, the only thing you'll be out of touch with is your money.

Again, my goal isn't to teach you the best SEO tactics. After all, tactics change daily and are often unique to each organization. Instead, my goal is to outline the philosophy behind search engine optimization, so you feel more confident having a conversation with your staff and vendors.

TAKE A DEEP BREATH

> If you've already hired an SEO expert and aren't seeing results, don't panic. Keep an open mind when reading through the tactics I share in this book and have a conversation with your SEO company.
>
> It also doesn't help that most people involved in SEO seem arrogant, which understandably puts people off, but maybe that's just my issue...

YOUR WEBSITE IS YOUR BOOK

I decided to write this book because I have digital marketing knowledge that I want to share with others. I feel my knowledge can help entrepreneurs and marketers make more educated decisions in their businesses.

For the purpose of this analogy, think of *my* book as *your* website.

Look at it this way: I have created a book that I believe will help a lot of people, in the same way that your business can help a lot of customers. I submit my book to Barnes & Noble (just like you might submit your website to Google Business to get it listed as a local business).

Once my book gets into Barnes & Noble, the manager of the bookstore is responsible for putting it in the right category. Now, imagine I chose to title my book something silly and obvious, like: *Kevin Wilhelm, the Book*. That would leave the bookstore manager with only one option: to put my book in the biography section. In that case, I'd have to bank on customers searching for me by name—the same way they'd search for books about Oprah Winfrey or Michelle Obama—in order to find me. However, I'm not naive. I know that I'm a relative nobody, especially compared to such big names. When competing against the likes of Oprah, I know that my book won't sell. And without sales, I can't help anyone.

To help people, I know it's important to name my book appropriately to attract the people I can serve. So instead of *Kevin Wilhelm, the Book*, I call it *Click: Transform Your Business through Digital Marketing*. As soon as you see the cover and title, you know what it's about. When you visit the marketing section of a bookstore or type "digital marketing" into Amazon, my book shows up. When I market my book in that way, I become part of the "digital marketing books for entrepreneurs" conversation, as opposed to the "biographies" conversation.

Google works in the same way. When Google indexes your website, it reads and determines what your company has to offer by looking through the content and being guided by "keywords," which are the terms on your site that allow Google to match searches to your business. If it's all about you instead of your company—or if you set your sights on ranking on a national level when you're not ready yet—you won't rank highly.

The problem is that most web developers lack SEO experience. Maybe you built your own website using a DIY website builder (such as Squarespace) or your cousin's nephew built it in his basement (why are these nephews always in basements?). In these cases, it's highly likely that your website doesn't rank for major keywords because you haven't told Google (or the bookstore manager) what you do and where you do it. Without those keywords, Google's algorithms will prevent you from showing up for relevant keyword phrases, and you'll only show up for your business name.

You'll be put in back storage with the rest of the forgotten companies.

DEFINE WHAT YOU DO

Effective SEO involves two main factors: onsite structural changes and offsite reputation building. Onsite changes involves shifting your website structure from telling Google *who you are* to *what you do* and *where you do it*. To do that, you have to update the building blocks of your website. That includes choosing relevant headlines (paragraph titles), creating meta-descriptions (behind-the-scenes page descriptions that only Google sees), page titles (what each page is called), and alt tags (image descriptions). When you create all of these, think about who you want to target.

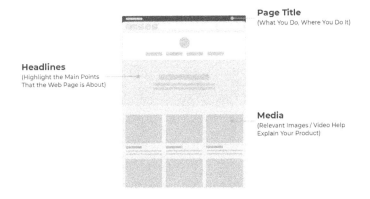

Page Title
(What You Do, Where You Do It)

Headlines
(Highlight the Main Points
That the Web Page is About)

Media
(Relevant Images / Video Help
Explain Your Product)

Be as specific as possible. Think carefully about location. For example, a lawyer based in New York might choose the keywords "lawyer New York," as this search phrase generates the most traffic. However, in a city like New York, you have to imagine that approximately 10 billion other lawyers use the same keywords. You'll get drowned out by your competition, and it'll be very difficult, timely, and expensive to rank highly.

However, if you specify that you're a personal injury lawyer in Manhattan, New York, you've increased your chance of success on two fronts:

- With this keyword phrase, you specify the type of law you practice and you specify a smaller geographical community. Google can now identify you as a personal injury lawyer in Manhattan. Because there is less competition involved in this search, your chance of showing up first in Google search results is much higher.
- As an extra bonus, the customers who find you through internet searches will be more qualified. You'll no longer have to turn away customers looking for divorce lawyers in Hoboken, New Jersey.

Don't underestimate the importance of narrowing down the search terms you want to rank highly for. As you narrow your focus to more specific communities and smaller subsets of your services, you can lower your investment and increase your chances of finding qualified prospects sooner.

> A good SEO company will do all of this for you. In theory, an SEO company should come to you already with recommendations for which keywords you should target and their plan for how they'll get you there.

AVOID KEYWORD STUFFING

Over time, Google has perfected its algorithms to reward content that is valuable for their users (i.e., people reading websites). However, in the last ten to fifteen years, there has been a big shift toward writing content for the people actually reading the website and not just for the search engines who are indexing it.

Imagine you're an auto mechanic in Los Angeles and you include this information in every paragraph of your website:

> Los Angeles auto mechanic Decker Auto is here to serve you. As an auto mechanic located in Los Angeles, it is Decker Auto's duty to serve everyone in the Los Angeles, California, community. Call Los Angeles auto mechanic Decker Auto at...

You (or your SEO manager) may think this is a good way

to show up higher on search results, but Google penalizes you for this behavior. It's called keyword stuffing, and it simply does not work anymore. Not to mention, it's annoying and (if you're like me) will leave you with a headache.

HOW MANY KEYWORDS ARE TOO MANY?

In the past, it was normal for keyword phrases to form 8–10 percent of your content. However, as time goes on, and Google's algorithms have gotten better, users have discovered that 8–10 percent is far too much—it reads like something a bot created. You want your content to feel natural for readers. As such, aim for 2–3 percent of your content to consist of your keywords.

The key to successful SEO isn't including your keywords on every page of your website and in every piece of content you create. You should only include your keywords to give context. You want your readers to know what you're about. Think of a keyword as similar to a chapter heading. The point of a chapter heading is to give your reader an idea of what the chapter will include. Any paragraph or page on your website should do the same thing.

LINK FARMING

When Google scans the web, every link it finds to your website is like a vote of confidence. It means that people care about your company enough to talk about it. Back in the days of keyword stuffing, another technique emerged that took advantage of this perception of links as a vote of confidence: link farming.

In essence, business owners paid link farmers to put links to the business owner's website on the farmer's web page. They had links to random businesses located all over the world. As you can imagine, these links didn't get clicked a lot because nobody visited link farms other than the farmers who put them there.

Eventually, Google's algorithms wised up (as they always do). Now the *quality* of links to your website has become more important than the *quantity* of links. While having links to your website is still a vote of confidence in your business, it's more important to provide high-quality content that encourages people to organically link to your site.

THE PROPER TECHNIQUE

The best way to rank highly is to focus on speaking to your customer effectively. That's what the algorithms are really looking for. One effective way to accomplish this is by creating individual pages for each service or product you offer.

Recently, I had a discovery call with a prospective client, Zulu Medispa. They are a medical spa that offers fifteen different spa services, including Botox and cool sculpting. They had a single page on their website that was just a long-form listing of all *fifteen* services they offer. Granted, their description of each service was excellent, but by housing all of it on one page they were trying to provide *everything* for *everybody* on a single page. They were depriving themselves of a better SEO opportunity, not to mention how ineffective this might be when trying to sell your services to a new customer. For this reason, their website struggled to rank at all.

A better approach would be to build a dedicated page for every service they offer. The page titles could be "Botox in Calgary, AB" for maximum SEO value.

Moreover, chances are that the people looking for Botox are a little older (35+). It's likely that more women will seek Botox than males. Therefore, that's the target audience: women, aged thirty-five-plus, looking to enhance their outward beauty.

As such, the web content should cater to those people. It should focus on the Botox services the spa offers, as well as how Botox works and the benefits Botox can provide to the customer. The website should detail how long a procedure will take and how many times a client is expected to come back. Obviously, the cost of a service is important to express. Many service companies also choose to include testimonials from customers in the area who have utilized the service. The more information and the more questions you can answer, the better the experience for your customers—which search engines love!

Just don't forget to include what your customers should do next. For example, do you want them to book a consultation? Then your call to action should lead them to do that.

With this type of framed content (meaning an individual page for each service you offer), you can ensure that you are one step closer in showing up in your prospective customers' Google search results.

YOUR HOMEPAGE

I often think of a website homepage in the same way I think of Grand Central Station in New York City—it's rarely the end destination; it's meant to help get your customers to what they're looking for as quickly as possible. Your homepage should be built to direct people to the crucial information on your website that will help a prospective customer make their decision.

Start by defining *who* you are and *how* you can solve your prospective customers' problems. Aim to show potential customers *why* they should do business with you. Offer them more information. Provide links to your services and descriptions of the company. Let them watch demos and direct them toward testimonials and reviews.

YOUR WEBSITE'S UNSUNG HERO: THE *"ABOUT US"* PAGE

This is going to surprise you. It shocked me when I first learned it...

The "About Us" page is one of the most visited pages on any small business website.

Shocking, right? That little page about you and your company—the one you thought nobody looked at—is perhaps the most popular page on your site. I don't know about you, but I didn't think consumers cared much about the "About Us" page. I figured they just found the contact information or maybe dived into your service pages, and then went about their business. As it turns out, your customers actually want to read about your company. They want to know who they're about to do business with. Who would've guessed?

This is just another one of those instances where real data can override instincts and assumptions. The great thing about digital marketing is that you can easily collect real data to help make strategic business decisions.

So why are your customers visiting your "About Us" page? They really do want to know who they're going to do business with. They have questions about you:

Do you believe the same things they believe?

Are you a family business, an individual, or some other group of people?

What do you stand for?

Don't treat your "About Us" page with minimal thought. Avoid slapping together a paragraph with your name, when you were established, and how many products you sell. Put serious effort into telling your unique story. Your story is one thing that truly separates you from your competition. Start by asking yourself, *Why would anyone want to do business with you in the first place?*

Are you the third generation in your industry, or are you the founding entrepreneur?

Do you have an amazing culture and a team full of unique personalities?

What makes your company unique within your field?

Have you won any unique awards or recognition for anything special?

Answering those questions will give you a great start in populating your "About Us" page.

One of the best examples I've ever seen: Yellow Leaf

Hammocks. Their "About Us" page tells a wonderful story of who they are and what their company is all about. They share their beliefs, their process, their employment practices, and their charitable contributions—all in an amazingly captivating way.

The company helps break the terrible cycle of poverty by creating sustainable job creation. They share the individual stories of some of their artisan weavers and the country in which they make the hammocks. It is both inspiring and motivational. It makes you want to buy a hammock from them. When your "About Us" page explains so much more than the details of your company and dives deeply into the reason your company exists, you can connect with your audience on an entirely different level.

PHOTOGRAPHY

This is where custom photography and videography can do wonders. Again, thousands of people will read this page to decide whether or not to do business with you. Adding a video profile of you and your team can do wonders to the effectiveness of your website.

You can have fun with the team pictures as well. One of the most engaging examples I've seen is a company that played hide-and-seek around the office. They took photos of each team member where they hid. Another great one: each person had a regular headshot but when you put your cursor over the image it switched to a funny face. They included everyone's bio, personal dreams, aspirations, and core values. It created a much more engaging "About Us" page that received comments from customers all the time!

Unfortunately, most businesses put little effort into their "About Us" page. They don't think anyone cares, so they write a single paragraph and move on.

I advise you to pay attention to your "About Us" page. Trust me. Not only does this page matter most to customers but also to your prospective employees, who want to know who they might work with. Instead of including a single job description, talk about who you are and what you stand for to attract the best employees.

I speak from years of experience. As an agency, we have attracted some amazing talent by talking about the unique things that make us who we are.

There is no ideal length for an "About Us" page, as long as you tell your story completely and honestly. The key is the longer you can get your users to stay on your website, the more pages they are likely to read. The more they read, the more valuable your website becomes.

ROOM FOR IMPROVEMENT

A website is *never* complete. There are always aspects you could improve. You might move your phone number to a different place on the homepage, change your content, or alter the required fields in a form.

> Whenever you add a requirement to fill out a field in a form, you'll see a reduction in how many people complete it. If you don't need a customer's phone number, don't ask for it. In my experience, if you remove the mandatory field of phone number and let customers give their email, conversion rates skyrocket. People feel uncomfortable with the idea that someone could call them at any time.

Analyze how people interact with your website. Know your conversion rates. Marketing agencies are super helpful in this regard because they report to you on these figures. In short, the more you understand about how people are interacting with your website, the more efficient and effective you can make it.

Adopt the mentality of improvement. Accept that your

website isn't as effective as it could be and constantly think about what you could change to make it better.

WRITE FOR ALL PERSONALITIES

Keep in mind that your website will be read by many people with completely different personalities. I see many websites where business owners or hired content creators appear to write content for themselves. For example, an analytical person will want countless lines of text, while a Type A personality wants short and concise content. You have to find out who your buyer is to best serve their personality type.

> You're not your buyer, and your buyer isn't you.

While writing great content helps with search engine optimization, you also want to make sure you write for different personality types. As such, utilize *opt-in content*. For example, you could have a headline that, when clicked on, displays more text below (we call this an accordion). This way, readers can consume information quickly and decide whether they want more or not.

Let's return to the Botox example. On the medical spa website, there might be a headline that reads, "Come in Every Six Weeks." Next to the headline could be an arrow button and a plus sign. When you click the arrow, you get several more paragraphs about why it matters to come in every six weeks. Maybe this time frame is recommended by a certain board or six weeks is the necessary time for your muscles to recover. Whatever the case may be, those two paragraphs will make all the difference for a certain type of customer—the type who wants to read more information than the next person.

Personally, I read websites quickly, and I'm more inclined to skim headlines. However, someone more analytical will want to understand *why* every six weeks is the recommended time frame. Such a customer wants to opt in for more content or more explanation of the service before they feel confident calling or booking a consultation.

HOW SALESY SHOULD I GET?

If your goal is for a customer to buy a product, it's appropriate to use sales language. Explain *why* you are better than other businesses out there. Outline the benefits of your product. Why should a customer buy from you?

Your website is your best salesperson. Rather than people in your business, your business works twenty-four hours a day and never takes a sick day. Most importantly, a website will *always* say what you want it to say. While a salesperson needs training and coaching, a website will constantly sell who you are and what you do, provided you invest in its script.

MAKE USE OF MULTIMEDIA

Videos can be very beneficial for SEO. People love videos,

and Google does, too. However, there are certain factors to take into consideration before you make as many videos as possible.

More important than anything else on your website—even more important than having good copy—is having a fast website. Speed matters. In fact, speed is one of the most important factors in SEO today. And self-hosting a video on your website is one of the quickest ways to slow down your site.

Therefore, the best practice for including videos on your site is hosting them through a third-party site, such as YouTube, Vimeo, or Wistia, then embedding the code onto your own website (your website developer handles this for you with minimal effort). It's the best of both worlds: you have great video content that doesn't slow your site down.

MOBILE FRIENDLY

These days, if your website isn't mobile friendly, there's a good chance it won't even show up when somebody searches for you on their phone—Google has now determined a separate algorithm for mobile search results.

The way your website looks on a desktop is different from the way it looks on a phone (this is called being *responsive*). Because of the modern mobile shift, people are more likely to access your website from a phone than a desktop. If you're in the rare category of desktop-only websites, chances are your website is receiving far less traffic than it ever did before, and you've been steadily losing business to competitors with better equipped responsive websites.

STEP INTO YOUR CUSTOMERS' SHOES

Every industry is different. Take the engineering industry as an example. In engineering, nobody makes decisions quickly. Anyone who visits the website of an engineering firm has probably been referred to them and is now trying to understand more about the firm, the projects they've done, and the experience they have. The sales life cycle is long, and therefore, the prospect is in no hurry to make a decision or to even reach out for more information. This customer is probably sitting at a desktop in their office performing research. In this case, the most important thing for the engineering company is to provide the prospect with a ton of content, including past projects, information about the team, and any accolades the company has earned. It's less important to have a large phone number present for the prospect to be able to call them immediately.

However, imagine later that day the same person searching for engineering is now trying to figure out why their furnace stopped running on a freezing-cold day. At that moment, they're probably standing in their furnace room in despair, fed up and needing help as soon as possible. They go on their phone to look specifically for a company that can show up and fix their furnace *immediately*. Their main priority, therefore, is determining availability and finding a phone number. The opportunity for a furnace repair company would be to highlight emergency, same-day repairs, and an easy-to-access phone number as soon as you visit their website from a phone.

In this example, you can see that the customer on the phone is in higher need. That customer doesn't care about the entire experience of the website. The information they are searching is relatively small in scope but high in importance.

Put yourself in your customers' shoes. Think about problems from their perspective.

Ask yourself: does our website *experience* reflect what our customers need from us in the moments that matter?

USE AN INTERLINKING STRATEGY

Say a customer with a completely broken furnace is on the furnace repair page of Action Furnace's website. If the website provides a link from the furnace *repair* page to a furnace *replacement* page, they could sell that customer a new furnace.

Look for similar opportunities to pull your customer along their journey to different pages on your website. As such, frequently link to your "About Us" page, as well as the pages for other products and services you offer.

Interlinking your pages will create a more robust experience for your customers. Remember, a successful webpage includes more than two paragraphs of content. You've created multiple pages on your website for a reason. Let the customer know that these pages exist and help them know what to expect when they get there by interlinking them frequently.

On every service page, you might also link to a review page. That way, you encourage unsure or skeptical customers to read what happy customers have to say about you. If customers are unsure about pricing, it might help to link to a financing page. Give them easy access to different pricing options. If you want a customer to know about your level of experience, link them to your "Portfolio" or "About Us" page.

Think of your website as a whole customer experience, not a collection of static documents without connection. When a customer browses your website, they are on a journey. How positive that journey ends up being is up to you.

A customer might only spend two minutes on your website. Use those two minutes to convince them to do business with you. The businesses that create the best online experience are the ones that will win the most customers.

AN INFORMATION LIBRARY

Over time, Action Furnace followed all of the steps outlined in this chapter to improve their search rankings. In doing so, one of the strategies was to build them an information library—a section of their website that housed valuable information that customers frequently asked. They have blogs on everything from *how an air conditioner works* to *the top 5 causes of furnace failure*. This content portrays them as the local online authority, and this authority is something Google absolutely looks for when deciding which websites rank in their search results pages.

When deciding which content to include in your information library, you'll want to know what content/information is being searched by your prospects already.

Google has tools online to help you perform keyword research. Marketing agencies can pull that together or even look internally within your own business for that competency. Ask yourself what questions are you being asked on a regular basis? Before they are asking an expert (you), chances are that they are typing in a similar search online to find the answer as well. The more targeted your content can be, the better chance you'll have at appearing in front of your prospects at the exact right time.

IT TAKES TIME

Picture the scene:

Someone goes onto Google, types in *your* industry and *your* city, and your company's website is the first one to show up. Imagine that feeling. I'm here to tell you it is possible, but it'll take time.

Write down a list of every product, service, and brand you offer. Think about the different ways someone might search for your company (do they search "furnace repair in Beverly Hills" or "furnace company 90210"? You need to know). Keep in mind that just because you rank well for one search, that doesn't mean you will rank well for all searches. No two people are the same, which means no two searching habits are the same either.

Your website can't appeal to everyone. Think about your ideal customer, think about what search phrases they might use, and build your website to cater to their needs, not your own. If you do that successfully and give it time to work, you'll build a search engine optimized website that doubles as your best salesman.

Don't expect to create a successful and perfectly optimized SEO website overnight, even if you work with an agency (which you should). It takes a long time for a quality website to come together, and even then, it's an ongoing process, not a "set it and forget it" asset in your business. You need to commit to creating the best and most robust experience.

CHAPTER 4

—

How to Harness and Get More Online Reviews

After you've created a great website, another way to improve SEO is through customer reviews.

These days, most companies are obsessed with having all five-star reviews. However, it's easy to forget that businesses are run by human beings. That means they're not perfect. For that reason, it's difficult to expect your online review profile to consist of only five-star reviews.

When I see a business with 100 percent five-star reviews, I tend not to believe it—something doesn't feel right. In my eyes, that business is trying too hard to make its customers believe that it is a five-star business, which, in itself, is not believable.

The ideal rating range for your business is between 4.5 and 4.9 stars. Not only is that a great range, but it's believable, too. In this chapter, I'm going to tell you how to respond to, harness, and get more online reviews for your company.

YOUR RESPONSE

You can absolutely have four-star reviews (with a couple of three stars thrown in), and it won't be the end of the world. What's more important than the review itself? How you deal with it.

One of the SEO triggers we've found is the responsiveness of business owners responding to their online reviews. Google looks to see if you are an active and invested business owner online. To be seen as active and invested, you should be responding to all of your reviews quickly. Say you have a social media page for your business, and someone asks you a question on the page. If you don't respond, it looks like you don't care. Invested business owners pay attention to what's going on. The businesses that respond to their customers via social media are more likely to provide a better experience for their customers. And Google sees that and values it.

Therefore, your response to reviews is just as important as the reviews themselves. Think of it as a two-way conversation. Nobody wants to be seen as an absent business owner. Be as present as possible.

How can you be as present as possible?

Subscribe to your reviews, whether they're on Google, Yelp, or Facebook. In that case, whenever somebody leaves a review, you get notified no matter where the review is left. Then, once you get notified of the review, respond. If you receive a compliment, thank your customer and close the loop on their experience. Express that you're glad they had a positive experience with your company. If someone asks you a question, answer it as quickly as possible.

That's the easy stuff. Now, what if someone has negative feedback for you? It's a whole different ball game.

By leaving a negative review, your customer is making their issue with your company public. That doesn't mean you have to *keep* it public. Once you see the negative review, acknowledge that that customer's experience doesn't align with your goals as a business. Make it clear that you will do everything necessary to rectify their situation. Offer to hear about their experience in more detail. And most importantly, provide them with a way to contact you offline.

I have witnessed too many business owners become petty by arguing with customers online. And I can understand where they're coming from. Obviously, it's frustrating to read a review that you feel is unfair, unrepresentative, or even a complete falsehood. However, by engaging in a *public* debate, you're forgetting about the potential repercussions that the argument could have on other customers.

Example Review:

> "My experience with your company was just horrible. I had to wait for what seemed like hours before anyone offered to help me, then they made a recommendation which was your most expensive product, then the product didn't work and finally when I tried to return the product, you refused to take it back. I would NOT recommend your company to anyone!"

Don't Respond like This (even though it'll feel good to):

> "After reviewing our surveillance tapes, we can definitively see that you waited less than 2 minutes when you arrived in our store, was greeted by a salesperson and spent 10 minutes going through our various products. You asked specifically for the product you purchased and then tried to return it once YOU broke it trying to put it together. Our return policy states that we cannot accept returns that are

damaged out of the packaging. We strongly recommend reading and following the instructions before trying to tackle the construction and installation of our products."

A response like this shows future potential customers that you are willing to argue in public and potentially embarrass your customers. While the response above might be accurate, it will hurt your brand as you will scare off future customers from wanting to interact with you. Instead, try a softer approach...

"Thank you for voicing your concern and sharing your frustrating experience. Every member of our company strives to provide an exceptional customer experience, and we take these stories very seriously. We would ask that you contact our store manager directly to share more details about your story so we can work with you to find a resolution."

This response shows that you care and reinforces your company values while not admitting any fault in the situation.

THE POWER OF YOUR SOCIAL CIRCLE

I genuinely believe that if (when) Facebook creates a search engine, it will be the most powerful in the world. Think about it: imagine if you could search for a restaurant near you and instantly saw which of *your friends* have eaten there, what they ate (with photos), and who enjoyed/didn't enjoy it. It would be so much more powerful than relying on strangers' reviews.

But that's just where we are in the overall internet review experience: we mostly rely on strangers we've never met.

> As we move forward and collect more information about users and connect our social media and digital platforms, our search results will become much more tailored to our specific needs.

TWO EXTREMES

Generally, customers leave reviews for one of two reasons: either their experience grossly exceeded their expectations or grossly fell below their expectations.

To help me qualify this, I think of a dinner party. Most people won't share their average customer experiences at a dinner party with their friends. For example, you probably wouldn't be eager to tell your friends about your morning visit to the grocery store, where you found the items you needed, waited in line for a normal amount of time, and received average customer service. (If this *is* you, I probably want to skip your dinner parties.)

However, imagine you went to the grocery store and

someone went out of their way to help you carry your bags (because you had your child with you) and afterward gave your child a balloon and a coloring pack. You'd likely share that experience. Equally, if someone at the grocery store was exceptionally rude and offensive toward you, you'd feel compelled to share that, too.

As a business owner, your goal is to think about ways to give customers positive experiences that they wouldn't expect. Instead of *fearing* that Yelp, Google Reviews, or Facebook can ruin your business, think like an entrepreneur: imagine everything is within your control and create the kinds of experiences that *make* people talk about you positively at the dinner table and online.

BE GENUINE

How many times have you had a deep conversation with an Uber driver? If you're like me, it happens all the time. In the span of a single car ride, you can find out everything about their family, dreams, and background story. You feel like you've made a genuine connection.

Now imagine you're getting out of the car and that same Uber driver you just connected with reminds you to give them a five-star review. Suddenly, you question everything. You wonder whether you made a genuine connection with them in the first place, or if they were just placating you to get a five-star review.

If you remind your customers to give you a five-star review, you risk them feeling like your service isn't genuine. Instead, rely on making genuine connections with your customers. The more genuine that connection, the more likely that customer will speak highly of you and leave you a review.

NO OBLIGATION

Here's how you get customers to leave reviews without feeling any obligation whatsoever.

When you meet a customer for the first time, ask them if they read any online reviews for your company prior to engaging with you. If they say yes, ask them if the reviews made an impact on their decision to choose you. Then, simply point out that those reviews matter a lot because they can impact the number of customers you get in the future.

After that, don't mention reviews again during the interaction. Instead, focus on the actual experience that you're providing for your customer.

Despite what some might say, I genuinely believe that people want to help other people. If a business satisfies my expectations as a customer, I want to help that company continue to satisfy other customers. I can do this by leaving them a positive review online.

Do everything you can so your customers don't feel *obligated* to review your services. Obligation doesn't work for anybody. For example, I didn't actually mind cleaning our house when I was a child. However, when my mom *asked* (forced) me to clean, I automatically hated it. I wanted cleaning to be a choice, not a chore. As soon as I was forced to clean, I looked for every reason not to.

Your customers go through a similar psychological response when you ask them to leave reviews. If they feel like writing a review, it feels good for them to take that initiative without being told to. However, as soon as they feel obligated, they might feel resentful.

WHAT IF I GET A NEGATIVE REVIEW?

If you receive a negative review online, I recommend trying to take it offline as quickly as possible. And no, I'm not saying you should call up Google in a huff asking them to remove the review. I mean you should take *the conversation* offline. When you receive a call from that customer, be thankful that they are giving you an opportunity to learn about their experience and how it went wrong. It doesn't matter if their review is factually accurate. What matters is that customer's *perception* of their experience.

Most people don't speak up when they have a bad experience, and when they stay silent, they deprive you of the opportunity to improve your customer's experience. Think about every time you've gone to a restaurant and eaten an undercooked or overcooked steak. How many times do you send it back relative to how many times you suck it up and eat it anyway, often telling the server that your food is "great"? My guess is that you won't complain.

Now consider the friend at your table who *does* complain. What happens? The waiter might bring out a new plate or take the dish off the bill to make your friend happy. That friend gave the restaurant an opportunity to delight them and may leave the business more satisfied than if everything had gone according to plan.

Similarly, when someone leaves you a negative review, they're giving you an opportunity to learn where your gaps in service are and giving you a chance to close those gaps.

When somebody leaves you a complaint, get on the phone and thank them for giving you a review in the first place. Listen to what they have to say. If the problem is out of your control, give them an explanation. Help that customer understand *why* their experience was the way it was. If you can rectify a problem, do it. If you can exceed their expectations and provide a solution that goes above and beyond, do it.

At the end of the conversation, ask if you have resolved their issue. Close the loop. Remember, you're not explicitly asking them to change their review. You're simply asking for their feedback in that moment. Think of yourself as nudging them toward a more positive review without actually asking for one. Otherwise, the entire interaction will feel like bribery. Use a closing statement similar to this: *"Mr. Customer, have we done enough today for you that you feel the review you left has been resolved? Great, thank you."*

In the world of business, the internet can be a wonderful tool. Through the internet, anyone can find your business at a moment's notice. However, the internet also allows people to write whatever they want to write, which is often out of your control.

As a business owner, focus on delivering the best experience possible to your customers. That's the best way to guarantee five-star reviews.

HARNESSING YOUR REVIEWS

Once you've built up enough positive reviews, it's time to incorporate them into your website. Moreover, consider incorporating good reviews into your marketing strategy, especially if they offer you a competitive advantage. For example, if your competitors have a lower Google rating than you, promote that on your *"About Us"* page or your social media platforms.

If what you do best is represented in your reviews, encourage people to read them. Put your money where your mouth is and make it easy for people by displaying positive reviews on your website.

TYPES OF REVIEWS

If you do get negative reviews, trust your customers to filter through them without you having to intervene and do it for them. For example, if I'm considering using a certain dentist and I see someone has left a one-star review about them, I read the review and decide whether or not the content of that particular review matters to me.

Say the customer expresses their annoyance that the dentist wasn't open on a Sunday. If I'm happy to visit the dentist on any day but a Sunday, that review doesn't deter me from doing business with that company.

However, if you notice that your business is getting negative reviews that are valid and relate to multiple aspects of your business, it may be time to make changes to your company.

For example, I had a client whose business included a network of properties listed on Airbnb. He ran these properties similar to a hotel. Essentially, customers had the corporate feel of a hotel with the convenience of an Airbnb. However, with that system, a customer had to first drive to a central office to pick up keys and then drive to the Airbnb, often paying more in Uber or cab rides from the central office to the Airbnb. Some customers didn't realize this was the procedure when they booked, so they'd show up at the Airbnb only to realize there was no way to get in. You can see how this would create a negative experience and lead to negative reviews.

What an amazing opportunity to listen to the reviews and implement strategic changes in the business to satisfy customer concerns.

As a business owner, you should aim to make your customers' lives as convenient as possible.

Low reviews give you an opportunity to understand how to improve your business. Think about it this way: if a customer takes the time to leave a poor review, your business clearly matters to them. That means you have an opportunity to get them to return to your company—as long as you make changes.

REVIEWS MATTER

Stay on top of your reviews. Harness the good ones, and don't let the bad ones freak you out. Go above and beyond for your customers and you'll see your positive reviews skyrocket.

Don't get me wrong, great reviews matter for your business. However, imperfect reviews are just as valuable. They serve as opportunities to improve your operations.

CHAPTER 5

———

Content Marketing

Content marketing is exactly as it sounds—creating various forms of content (written, video, photography, social media, speaking, etc.) that either educate or entertain your intended audience. Content marketing is your opportunity to tell the world your company's story.

As such, content marketing is all about the story. The first step in successful content marketing is deciding what story you want to tell.

What is your message?

What is your value proposition?

What problem are you trying to solve for your audience?

All entrepreneurs should want to help educate their clients on what they do and the value they bring with their business. The content you can create has an amazing opportunity to help your audience solve problems. You likely have customers coming to you every day asking similar questions, asking for your help to solve similar problems. By creating content that answers these questions and solves their problems, you create an authority about yourself and differentiate your business from everyone else you compete with.

Some businesses choose to entertain their audience through their content creation. Entertainment could be defined in various forms: humor, inspiration, motivation, among many more. In most cases, businesses utilizing this strategy are intentionally trying to create emotional ties between their brand and their audience.

A great example is from WestJet, a Canadian airline that approached the market differently than their competitors. Every year they create a holiday video where they orchestrate an incredible moment of wonder. One year, they asked guests what was on their holiday wishlist before they got onto their departing flight and by the time their guests arrived at their destination, they had gone out, purchased, and wrapped all of the gifts. Santa met them at the terminal and handed them all out to the passengers. Millions of YouTube views later, they are building their brand through accomplishing the impossible and pulling on the heartstrings of people everywhere.

HOW TO DO CONTENT MARKETING

Content marketing can be done in many ways, including:

- Infographs
- Explainer videos
- Webinars
- Training events/workshops
- Podcasts
- Writing a book

There are so many ways to get content out to an audience. Naturally, content creators will feel comfortable with a different medium and will gravitate toward a way that works best for them. When creating your own content for the first time, start where you're comfortable. As you build more content, look at ways to expand your platforms, reach, and mediums. Your expansion of content will result in an expansion of your audience who consumes it.

When deciding how to use content marketing in your own business, think about your target customer.

How does your audience consume information?

Next, look at the internal capabilities in your company. For example, you might be a great interviewer with loads of ideas. In that case, you could host a podcast. If you present well physically, video marketing could be your prime medium.

Consider your product as well. If your product requires training, you might want to create webinars explaining how your product works—this is an interactive way to connect to an audience.

In our company, we put on an annual marketing conference because one of our partners is an amazing event planner. We take advantage of the fact that event planning is a key competency within our organization.

We also have a video production team to make videos and copywriters to write blogs. Our graphic designers create infographics and ads. Look carefully at the strengths within your company to determine your own content-marketing strategy.

When it's all said and done, a large part of determining your strategy will come down to trial and error. Start by determining the type of content you believe will be valuable, but be open to trying different mediums, and see how your audience reacts to each one.

STEVE JOBS'S STORY

Think back to when Steve Jobs introduced new products through keynote addresses. By making those announcements on stage, he was able to broadcast his brand. For example, the way he explained the release of the iPhone in 2007 was a perfect example of him showcasing how his product was better than others on the market. Like a true entrepreneur, he carefully considered the best medium for content marketing. Apple could've put out a press release, attended trade shows, or launched a new phone like any other cell phone manufacturer, relying on salespeople and advertising to explain the product. But by hosting product launches streamed by people all over the world, Steve Jobs could tell the *story* of his product in exactly the way he wanted to tell it. Visit YouTube and watch the original iPhone keynote address—it's crazy to watch the reaction of the crowd.

OUR STORY

My company does a lot of content marketing. For example, we publish a monthly blog to advise companies on how to market better internally. Alongside this blog, we post videos on our social media channels. We visit different cities, hosting two-hour workshops to train people to do better marketing. We have also done webinars, and I have appeared on many podcasts.

The overall aim of these different mediums is to *educate*. In other words, our content marketing isn't designed to sell. We don't try to convince people to hire us. Instead, we teach people how digital marketing works and why it'll help them. Through education, we hope to be seen as experts in our field.

And who wouldn't want to hire an expert to do the job for them?

For example, Hard Rock Developments, one of our clients, sells beautiful DIY concrete products. Their products are designed for do-it-yourselfers and contractors. One of their main marketing strategies is to host free workshops on how to utilize their products. For free, customers can learn how to make their own countertop. While the company's content marketing is education, customers are simultaneously encouraged to use their products.

That's the power of creating content that comes from a place of genuinely trying to educate and help your customers.

BE A GUEST

Before you can be a guest on a podcast or a blog, you have to identify what you want to say. If someone were to interview you, what would your value proposition be?

There are so many people out there creating their own content. Podcast hosts are constantly looking for guests to provide them with information. Once you identify your story and how you can help people, reach out to the people around you. Provide them with the content they need.

All it takes is a Google search. Start by compiling a list of podcasts in your city. Reach out and send an email to introduce yourself. Describe what you could discuss in an interview and how this would be valuable for their readers, listeners, or viewers.

To find podcasts, I began by approaching my local chamber of commerce. I expressed that I was willing to provide free digital marketing advice for CEOs and business owners. As it turned out, they had a CEO peer group, so we scheduled for me to give a one-hour digital marketing 101 masterclass. Out of the five people in that room, two became clients of mine. From that single talk, I have generated six figures in revenue.

I tell you this to point out how easy it can be to find these opportunities to share your knowledge with your community.

SHARE VALUE

If you take anything from my experience, let it be that you have value that you can share with your audience. My audience consists of entrepreneurs, business owners, and marketers. Your audience might be different.

Whoever your audience is, recognize that you can provide something valuable to them. Consider how you can provide that value for free, in exchange for expertise and thought leadership, for example. Think about interesting ways to reach your audience and provide them with the right message.

- Know your content.
- Understand your audience.
- Get your message out there.

Identify the people who you want to represent your company. Maybe your business development leader is great at sales and can create helpful content for your customers. In our organization, we get everybody we believe has expertise and can offer value to our audience to create content.

For example, everybody in our company has written a blog. Moreover, every employee creates a preview video to explain the point of their blog and how it can help customers. Afterward, we have somebody internal dedicated to distributing and promoting it.

BLOGGING

The most straightforward advice I can offer about blogging is this: identify the questions your audience will be typing into a search engine and create a blog to answer them.

Let's consider the childcare space. This is an industry I know well, as I used to run the marketing for a national childcare company called BrightPath Kids. Who's the audience of a childcare center? The parent of a new child. At the end of her maternity leave, a mother needs to find care for her child. However, she also has a million other thoughts running through her head, like vaccinations, bathing, sleeping, and getting her child to eat their vegetables, to name a few.

My guess is that most new mothers would benefit from a parenting blog that can help answer their questions. If you're in the childcare space, you could probably find someone with enough expertise to run a blog with tips, tricks, and parenting hacks.

When my wife and I were new parents struggling to get our newborn to sleep, we would try just about anything, including searching online for some advice. If I had found an article written by a local childcare provider, I might have considered them as our primary provider when we needed childcare. This was part of my overall strategy for BrightPath, and it served us well for years.

By creating content that is valuable to your audience, you create an opportunity for a prospective customer to find you. This all contributes to building a positive brand impression.

As previously mentioned, start with one medium you're comfortable with and then expand to new platforms. We took those blog articles and expanded our reach into radio campaigns. We had one of our childcare center directors on air, providing childcare tips, like how to get a child to fall asleep and unique ways to get your child to eat their vegetables. These were essentially public service announcements through the form of radio ads. Every two weeks, we switched one ad out for another. While we used advertising to get the message out, it was valuable content that helped form a positive impression of the brand and brought more customers through the door.

FULL CIRCLE

It's difficult to measure direct ROI for a blog, because you're aiming to create an *impression* and value. While customers might discover you through advertising or word of mouth, the valuable articles you publish will convince them to call you.

Although we're able to track marketing better now than ever before, it's also becoming harder to attribute direct correlation between *which* marketing efforts have which impact.

Content marketing is not about achieving an expected ROI today. Instead, aim to establish authority and expertise through your content over a long period of time. That way, when someone is considering you and your company, their choice is made easier.

THE COMPETITION

If your competitors aren't creating strong content, you stand out even more as competent, unique, and special in your field.

If your competitors *are* creating content, don't ignore it. Instead, make an effort to understand it. Investigate their content and study it.

How long are their blogs?

How often do they come out?

Are they topical?

Are they opinionated or controversial?

Is their advice different than the advice you would give?

You have two options when facing your competitors: either you choose to go head-to-head and create a competing type of content, or you recognize a gap in content creation within your industry. If nobody in your space is making a podcast, that might be a great opportunity to start a podcast yourself, for example.

CREATING A PODCAST

Before you create a podcast of your own, make sure you know your audience. The more specific your messaging, the more qualified the group you'll reach (which is actually a great thing).

> The same applies for all types of content marketing: the more niche, the better.

Quite often, the person who runs the podcast is the host, and they facilitate conversations with other experts. Through the podcast, they bring together a network of guest speakers. In doing so, they diversify their messaging and reach a wider audience, and that will help promote their brand.

Now, there are downsides to this approach. When you invite a guest on your podcast, you're creating a platform for *them* to promote *themselves*. In that case, you're splitting the influence of the podcast.

Alternatively, when you are the only person on the podcast, it's all about you. You can control the message, how it's delivered, and you're fully in control of promoting your company. The downside here is that you need *a lot* of content to talk about.

Once you decide the format of the podcast, decide whether you want to post daily, weekly, or monthly. Do you have enough content to post daily? Will your audience become disengaged if you only post monthly? Ask yourself those questions to zero in on your ideal frequency.

How long is your podcast run time? I've heard some podcasts that are under ten minutes and others that are over two hours. Think about your audience's attention threshold and decide your length from there (also consider your stamina and how long you can talk for).

You won't get it all perfect at first. You'll learn lessons over time. But no matter what mistakes you make, start off being as professional as possible. Invest in the right microphone; create the right environment. A noisy office is not the best place to record. If you invite guests, make sure they're well prepared. Warm up with them.

Whatever you do, make sure it sounds professional. The production value of your content represents your company. If there are errors in your articles, videos, or podcast episodes, people will immediately associate this with the perception of your brand.

WEBINARS VS. WEBCASTS

Webinars and webcasts are two other great ways to create content for your company. They're very similar but have a simple distinction:

- A webinar is typically a live one-way conversation with your audience.
- A webcast generally has similar content but is pre-recorded.

Keep in mind that anything can happen during a webinar. Personally, I don't like doing webinars because I have to rely on technology to get the content out to my audience *live*. I have to trust that slides will be ready and that notifications from my computer won't sound in the middle of a live webinar. A webcast, on the other hand, allows you to do different takes and lets you edit and perfect before anyone sees it.

> Trust me, I speak from experience. Once during a live webinar, when my iPhone was connected to iMessage, my friend sent me a message about the one-night stand he'd had the night before. That message was seen by the fifty potential customers on my webinar. Naturally, I became distracted...and so were the prospects who saw the message.
>
> That's the technological risk of a webinar.

FREE OF CHARGE?

As a business owner, you need to decide how much of your content to give away for free. With free content you can reach a wider audience. However, by charging for content, you're more likely to reach the *right* audience: people who want and need your services.

Personally, I have debated charging for seminars and webcasts. It's a difficult decision. We know that more people will have access to our content if it's free, and it's hard to predict how many people would pay for an article or podcast. At the same time, charging for your content will help offset the costs of creating it and provides your audience with an inherent value. "You get what you pay for" is always a statement that sticks with me. If my content is free, will people believe it to be valuable? If I charge for it, how could it not be valuable?

No matter what path you choose, your content should only be *part* of a wider marketing strategy. If you're charging people for it, be sure that what you have to say is so valuable that it should be paid for.

If you do choose to charge for content, I still recommend offering some free content, too. Think of this as a taster to help people understand why they should buy from you.

BAD BLOGGING HABITS

Nobody wants to read a boring blog. A blog should provide value for an audience, not exist solely to boost your ego. Some businesses treat blogs like newsletters, updating audiences about their advancements as a company. Nobody cares about that.

A blog should be about establishing you as an authority; it should aim to solve problems. Avoid talking about yourself too much. Instead of explaining what's happening in your business, think about how you can help solve people's problems.

A HIGH-QUALITY STEAK

There's a reason why fast-food restaurants have hard chairs and bright-lighting colors, while fine-dining restaurants have comfortable chairs and low-mood lighting. Not only do fast-food chains want you in and out, the perception of fast food is that it is cheap. Nobody expects a fast-food restaurant to offer high-end seating.

In fine dining, the production value matters because it dictates price value. As a customer, you know when you're being served an amazing steak compared to when you're being served a $6.99 steak sandwich.

In a restaurant, your marketing is the entire ambience of the experience you create. Say I go to a restaurant specifically to order a steak. The marketing begins long before that steak reaches my mouth. The lighting, the waitstaff, the chairs, and everything else all contribute to the experience. The meal is just the end product or service being delivered.

Through your content, you're setting the stage for the quality of your product. This also applies for customer service, your website, and the way you answer the phone. Until a customer has actually tried your product, the only way you can influence them is by presenting your brand in the way you want to.

A brand is the culmination of every interaction that your company makes with your audience. Think carefully about the messaging, articles, and videos surrounding your brand. Aim for high production value. If the production is low quality, the design is lackluster, or there are spelling mistakes in your marketing collateral (brochures, handouts, etc.), this determines the perceived level of quality your customers will receive in return.

Imagine you sit down in the steakhouse expecting a high-end experience. Then, you get your wine, and the glass has lipstick on it. You think it's a fluke, until you see the smudge on your fork. Immediately, your experience at that restaurant has been devalued. The steak could be the best in the world, but if the restaurant business doesn't "market" properly up to that point, the customer is lost before they ever get to taste the food. You may lose your customer before they ever get a taste.

LET IT EVOLVE

The first piece of content you create won't be your best work. Don't worry. It's also the one that will be seen the least.

Even if you work extremely hard, you probably won't see a lot of comments, likes, or shares at the beginning. Don't be discouraged. While people don't know who you are yet, that content remains available forever.

As you grow your audience, you'll reach more people who will go back and read your previous content. It might even take a year before someone shows interest.

But before you release anything, have realistic expectations about what you want that content to do. Is it intended to drive in new leads and generate a huge ROI? If so, it needs to be high quality.

Alternatively, you might use your content to become a thought leader. In that case, you need even more patience. This type of content marketing will help increase awareness about your brand and retain customers longer, but give it time—awareness now, deals later.

THE GRIND PAYS OFF

The first step to creating good content is believing that

you have value. You're in business for a reason. Clearly, your product or service is valuable.

Take it from me: you do have value. Now you just need to share it. Find a medium that resonates with you and your business and put your content out there.

If you believe in yourself and the solutions that you can offer your customers, your grind will pay off.

CHAPTER 6

Email Marketing

Awesome news! Your business is sitting on a gold mine. That's right—a gold mine. I don't care what industry you're in or what business you own or manage. If you are involved in a business, then you are sitting on a gold mine.

Even better? You have *all* the equipment you need to access that gold, you just need to know where to look. Where is this gold you ask? Your company is sitting on a database of past and current customers, prospects, and partners. The gold comes from the potential for these customers to buy from you again.

Most businesses spend too much energy looking for their *next* customer. Instead, you need to spend more energy on your past and current customers.

Now, most of us wrongly assume that because someone has purchased from us in the past, they'll be loyal to us for the rest of their lives. That's not true. Those relationships don't just happen—they need to be nurtured—earned—continuously.

We've all heard the old saying: it's cheaper to retain a customer than it is to find a new one. That's absolutely the truth. But how many customers do you already have in your database who are either one-time customers who could buy more from you, or were repeat customers a few years ago and haven't purchased from you since? Also, how many people have you connected with who weren't ready to be customers years ago but with changes in their needs or your offerings, are ready now?

And the million-dollar question:

How many email addresses have you collected from your customers?

We focus on growth and acquisition but rarely look at the opportunities that already exist in our past and current customer database. How do you go after that opportunity—how do we mine that gold?

Email marketing.

HOW TO USE EMAIL MARKETING

Now, some of your most loyal customers—past, present, and future—haven't given you their information yet. Just because they like your products or services doesn't mean you actually have their emails. Your first goal is to gather their emails (or their phone numbers, which is more important if you can send them text messages).

Text message marketing and email marketing go hand in hand.

How do you collect their contact information?

Simple: just ask.

Have a field for their email and phone number on your intake form, your outgoing form, and in your content marketing. For example, if people want to sign up for your newsletter, ask them for their email address. If your customer transactions occur in your retail store, just ask them at point of sale.

State explicitly that you won't use it to spam them—you just want to communicate with them. If you can, find a reason why they might want to share their email address: email receipts, coupons, offers, appointment reminders, etc., are all great ways to incentivize your customers to provide their contact info.

BE SPECIFIC

The more specific your email marketing is, the more effective it will be.

Your first instinct might be to think broadly and reach out to as many people as possible. Obviously, it's the least amount of work to send one email out to everybody. But that doesn't mean every customer cares about that particular email.

The more irrelevant your messaging, the more likely customers are to unsubscribe. Speak to particular audiences with specific messages.

Imagine one of Action Furnace's customers just bought a new furnace. The last thing they need is an email offer for a new furnace, especially if they're being offered a better price than what they paid. This is a fear of most businesses I talk to—but there are ways to avoid this! Create audience lists based on the buying behavior of your customers. When a customer buys a furnace, they need to be moved from a nurturing prospect list to a converted sale list. Your customer management systems should be set up to help you accomplish creating these audience lists.

Now, imagine a customer who bought a furnace and hinted at an interest in an air conditioner. A company engaged in email marketing would email this customer about buying an air conditioner. An effective email would be personalized. It would identify them as an existing customer and provide them with a special offer. If that customer had a positive experience with their furnace installation, they'll feel excited about the prospect of buying from the same company.

If another customer had duct cleaning done on a twenty-year-old furnace (about the age that a furnace should be looked at for replacement), *that* person should be getting emails about new offers on furnaces, not the person who just bought a new furnace.

MAP OUT CUSTOMER JOURNEYS

Imagine you own a kid's laser tag center. Because parents have to sign waivers in order for their kids to play, you have the email address of every parent who brings their kid to your business (along with that child's birth date).

Most parents start planning their kids' birthday parties thirty to sixty days in advance (and if you're my wife, then you're planning three years ahead). An effective example of email marketing would be to create an automated sequence that sends out an email with a birthday party offer sixty days prior to their child's birthday. Not only is this email sent out to the right person at the right time, but it also contains the right message.

This type of marketing doesn't need to be overly complicated or even automated. You could keep an Excel spreadsheet ordered by days of the year. Next to each day, you have contact information for the parent whose child has a birthday that day, and you'll send them an email sixty days before that date. Ultimately, this will only take five to ten minutes a day, but it'll have a big payoff if you can fill your schedule with birthday party bookings.

LESS IS MORE

In the contents of the email, be specific. If you're offering a customer something, highlight the offer. Make it clear what customers should do next.

Make sure the customer fully understands the offer and what they should do next.

If Action Furnace has a specific offer on air conditioners, customers should know that they have to call before a certain date to book a consultation (and if you have to list terms and conditions for your products, link to them on your website to avoid loading an email with unnecessary information).

Personalized emails make a huge difference. Include your customer's name, if possible:

Dear (Insert Customer's Name),

This is (Insert Employee Name) from (Insert Business Name).

I was thinking about you the other day and remember you mentioned you might need an air conditioner. I'm reaching out to see if you'd be interested in our offer.

This email can either look like it's written by an actual person, or it can be done up with professional videos and images. Different messages should have different formats.

WHEN EMAIL MARKETING HURTS

While email marketing can do wonders for a brand, sending too many emails can hurt your business. No customer wants to receive two emails a day from their best friend, let alone a random company they bought from once. If you don't have anything important to say, don't say it. Irrelevant emails will cause customers to unsubscribe.

If a customer stays on an email subscriber list, they expect to get something in return. The expectation is that the subscription will provide some value. This value could come in the form of customer service, like appointment reminders or invoice receipts. Otherwise, this value is likely a marketing offer that customers wouldn't get without their email subscription (a new product announcement, coupons, promotions, etc.).

ROOM FOR IMPROVEMENT

In email marketing, it's important to understand the metrics that matter. First, you should understand how many customer email addresses bounce back—as in, how many emails do you send to incorrect or dead email addresses?

Is your email list clean?

Using a service called NeverBounce (with which I have

no affiliation but use myself), you can upload your email list and find out which addresses are active. That way, you can see which emails are actually delivered and which bounce back.

Second, it's important to see how many emails are opened. If a customer doesn't open an email, you have no chance of delivering the message you want to deliver.

Consider your open rate carefully. Think about how you can get people to open an email. The subject line and the sending email address are important here. For example, it might make a difference whether your emails are sent from a receptionist, the marketing team, or you as the business owner.

While I'd love to provide you with a set formula for success, there isn't one. You have to test what works for you. For some businesses, a company-wide marketing email address might work. Some companies might have a higher open rate if emails are sent from you, the owner, directly.

Play with different subject lines, too. For example, you could send half of the emails with one subject line and half with another to see which one gets a higher open rate. Over time, you'll learn what makes your customers open an email. This is called variable testing and is a common technique when optimizing your performance. Test two variances for higher performance, keep the higher performer, and try another test. This is where marketing can become a lot of fun.

HAVE FUN

Tinker with your content and your subject lines. And when customers are opening your emails, find a way to track their response.

Imagine you run a pizza place, and you email your entire database an offer to receive a free appetizer, valid this Thursday only. Calculate how many people claimed the offer. Let's say you received thirteen claimed offers (giving away thirteen free appetizers), but fifty-six people opened the email. Track the conversion rate (23 percent) and use that number as a baseline to compare future campaigns against.

Say you have two subject lines. One is "Free Pizza until 6:00 p.m.," and the other is "We Still Have an Offer for You." The first subject line gets a 70 percent open rate while the second gets 20 percent. Clearly, "Free Pizza until 6:00 p.m." gets people to open their emails. If those two emails had identical offers once the email was opened, then you would know that the *subject line* is what drove more pizza sales. It had nothing to do with the content of the email or the offer itself. In this case, the subject line matters.

Alternatively, you could play with different offers and test which one sells more. One offer might be "Buy One Get One Free" while the other is 50 percent off any pizza. Track which order is more successful. It's important to remind you here that only one variable should ever be tested at once. If you run two experiments at the same time, how will you know which variance was more effective, which experiment actually drove results?

Have fun and experiment. Digital marketing is a journey toward finding the optimal equation, and you can't get there without playing around.

Just remember: email marketing has huge potential for your business. By sending the right number of emails containing the right message to the right people, you'll unlock a huge segment of customers you might have left untapped before.

THE DIFFERENCE IN MARKETING FOR E-COMMERCE AND BRICK-AND-MORTAR STORES

To be clear, there's a difference between using email marketing for your storefront business and email marketing for your e-commerce business. In a brick-and-mortar-style business, email marketing should be sparse and valuable enough to keep your subscribers continuing to subscribe. For e-commerce businesses, the strategy is totally different. I'm probably not going to unsubscribe from my favorite online clothing store if they send me emails because I like to shop there and will wait to see when new clothes arrive or go on sale. I just wait for the right offer at the right time. However, I don't want to receive daily emails from my local printing company or dentist office. So if you own a non-e-commerce business, do NOT look at online retailers as an example of what to do for your business.

ONE KEY MESSAGE

The emails you send out should have one key outcome you're going for. You want people to read something, buy something, or sign up for something. When you ask people to do all three, they get confused.

THE RIGHT TOOLS

The right tools are out there to do effective email marketing:

- Constant Contact: a popular email provider that allows you to build simple email campaigns to your database

- MailChimp: a direct competitor to Constant Contact, with similar functionality
- HubSpot: one of the most popular marketing automation platforms in the world, allowing marketers to create automated campaigns, landing pages, email campaigns, etc.
- ActiveDEMAND: a dynamic marketing automation platform built for agencies and enterprise clients. This software is very robust and customizable to your campaign goals.

Use them. And get creative with your email campaigns, while you're at it. You might send customers a thank-you for doing business with them after a year. You could send an email celebrating Flag Day or Presidents' Day. You might send them a birthday wish, gift, or offer. Make your emails thoughtful. Stand out to your customers.

A friend of mine, Andrew Obrecht, runs a boutique chain of fitness studios called YYC Cycle. Every email comes from the studio, except on a customer's birthday, when the owner sends a personalized birthday message. Although this email is automated, people think he's actually sending it himself, and they often reply expressing their gratitude. Acts like this are the reason someone would join a boutique gym instead of a chain gym: personalized emails create a real sense of community.

CAPITALIZE ON TRENDS

If you sell anything online, take advantage of key dates like Black Friday. Think of when customers are most ready to buy and start creating a strategy.

If you don't usually sell online, you can still capitalize on an online trend. For example, an optometrist could have a Black Friday sale on frames or contact lenses. A tire company could have a sale on a complete set of tires. A real estate company could offer a one-day discount on commissions.

As a business, you are sitting on a gold mine. Attack that gold with a strategic plan. Segment your audience, create specific email messaging, and track your results. Also, don't be afraid to test headlines, subject lines, and offers. Dig up that gold. You just might discover your own version of alchemy in the process.

CHAPTER 7

———

Video Marketing

Picture the scene. You're watching cable TV, and a scheduled commercial comes on. What do you do? You might be tempted to say you fast-forward and skip through commercials. That's what we *used to do*. I would argue that the vast majority of people use that time now to go on their devices and scroll through social media.

Traditionally, TV advertising has cost more money per impression than any other medium. This isn't because it has the greatest reach, but because it stimulates two of our five senses: sight and sound. By making two brand impressions at the same time, commercials become twice as effective because they're more memorable.

However, traditional TV advertising does present a few problems. First, people are watching fewer commercials every day. Not only can we record programs and skip commercials, but TV streaming has become more widely available. For example, I've purchased the NBA League Pass App for the past couple of years. When the game is on timeout, I watch the in-arena entertainment rather than commercials. Naturally, this means there are fewer opportunities to be shown commercials.

With the decrease in television's effectiveness, how are you going to harness the power of video for your business?

THE POWER OF DEVICES

Today, video marketing is primarily consumed on tablets and phones, which creates a much more intimate viewing experience. While our TVs are typically fifteen feet away from us, a device is six to twelve inches away from our face.

For most of us, a device is our most important physical asset. Ask yourself this question: what would you notice is missing first—your mobile phone or your child? This may be funny, but it's not a joke.

As a brand, you can still make a visual and audio impression simultaneously, despite cable's fall from dominance, but that impression is now being delivered through other platforms, like Facebook, Instagram, YouTube, Snapchat, and Vimeo. Cable stations *wish* they had such popular platforms.

Aside from your cable news stations, very few people are loyal to television channels or networks—they're loyal to shows. Really, they're loyal to *content*. I mean, how many people absolutely love CBS and will sit down to watch the network all night, regardless of the programs being shown? It's a crazy notion, but with YouTube, that's exactly what is happening. People are sitting down all night to watch content being created by their favorite content creators.

On networks, content decisions are made by producers in the hopes viewers watch it. On YouTube, the viewer truly decides what's worth watching by searching for what they want to watch. So if you create quality video content, people will find it, watch it, and share it. You might experience a tenfold increase in the number of brand advocates you have.

IT'S IN YOUR HANDS

I want to debunk the myth that video production is expensive.

The more popular video production has become in marketing, the more people there are creating videos. As such, the price of video production has naturally gone down. Five years ago, it was quite expensive for our agency to produce a video. Today, not a week goes by that I don't get approached by freelancers charging far less than I was used to paying historically. As the price continues to decrease, the production value also increases. Cameras are more readily available at a higher quality, and so you don't need the absolute best and most expensive equipment to make a quality production. GoPro made an entire video commercial with a GoPro. Similarly, Apple filmed an entire commercial on an iPhone. Both were amazing!

The cost of a good camera is no longer prohibitive to creating content. Additionally, there are more editing softwares available now, making content easier to create than ever before.

Think about all the people creating content on YouTube. These videos are filmed, edited, and self-published directly by the YouTubers themselves. To create a video, you no longer have to hire a production company. The tools are in your hands—if not directly, then by someone you can hire for far less than you think.

A LONG ROI

Video production is an investment with a long ROI. In my company, a promotional video I created five years ago is still being watched today in our sales process. When people decide to do business with me, they still comment on the impact that video had on their decision.

If you've ever heard of Dollar Shave Club, chances are that their launch video had something to do with it (their first video was an absolute viral success and is still being watched by millions of people). Think about how many adolescent men start shaving every year and, therefore, become prospective customers. Countless sixteen-year-olds on YouTube still come across that video each day and become Dollar Shave Club customers. Although that video was made years ago, it will continually provide ROI for years to come.

Amortize the cost of your video over the lifetime that someone could possibly watch it. Videos only become expensive when they're being created for short-term purposes. For example, you might create a video for a specific weekend sale in February, which you can't use again. However, timeless videos, which you can reuse, are one of the best investments you can make as a company.

BMW'S "THE HIRE"

In the early 2000s, BMW developed an amazing marketing concept. They created eight short films, each approximately ten minutes in length, with celebrities like Clive Owen, Madonna, Guy Ritchie, and Don Cheadle. These videos showcase the features of the BMW brand, but more importantly the aspirational lifestyle that BMW might provide.

Clearly, these videos have a high production value. BMW brought in huge stars and paid millions of dollars to get their brand message across. They generated millions of views on YouTube and continue to get watched to this day.

$100 OF MCDONALD'S IN TWENTY-FOUR HOURS

There are various strategies for making a video. You could make a video for entertainment value, like BMW. Their videos are brand aspirational, showing the performance of a BMW in action. Alternatively, you could educate your audience by talking about your product. Whatever path you choose, the angle you take with your video marketing depends on how you want your brand to be perceived and the value you can bring your audience.

No single strategy works for every company. Our company has used video to create a ninety-second explainer video about our company model (still shown to prospects today), and also invested in a prank video where they tried to embarrass me with a phony client trying to sell me his "ummy" idea (visit the POD Marketing YouTube channel to learn more).

In my favorite video, I ran an employee challenge where three members of our staff were challenged to eat $100 of McDonald's in twenty-four hours. The point was to test and showcase how different employees would tackle the challenge according to their roles and skillsets. For example, we were interested in how a creative designer would approach the challenge compared to a marketing scientist and marketing strategist. We viewed this as a way to show off the type of people we have in our company and a chance to show that we don't take ourselves too seriously.

A customer has no way of knowing an agency is effective before working with them. By creating a video like the McDonald's challenge, we hope to encourage prospective clients to work with us because we think differently.

> To view the challenge and the results, as well as the other videos mentioned above, search for *POD Marketing McDonald's Challenge* on our YouTube channel. It's completely worth it.

THE MARKETING STAGE

Once your video is created, upload it to all the video sites you can. Post it on Facebook, YouTube, and Vimeo. Find a place for it on your website and email it out to your subscribers, too.

If you put your video on YouTube, you can create an

advertising campaign around it. I believe online ads should be kept to fifteen seconds or less. Have a strong brand message and a call to action, and promote your video in the geographic areas most desirable to you.

Action Furnace has a strong brand promise to repair furnaces the first time out, or their customer doesn't pay. As their marketing team, we thought about how we could market their tagline as a funny branding play. We created a video speculating how other industries might use the guarantee "fixed right or it's free," but it wouldn't quite matter the same.

For example, we staged a scenario in a vasectomy clinic. A man walks in with a pregnant wife or girlfriend, and the doctor gives him his $100 back. Clearly, the $100 refund doesn't matter to that man at that point. The tagline "fixed right or it's free," while it technically works, doesn't really have an impact on his situation. At Action Furnace, that guarantee *does* matter and *does* have an impact. Customers want to make sure their furnace is fixed for cold nights. Since we put that video on YouTube, it has had over 250,000 views, which is impressive for a local business (search for *vasectomy clinic action furnace*).

While everybody wants to create viral videos, you can't predict whether or not a video will go viral. The best you can do is create videos that are valuable for you and your audience and hope they catch fire.

THE FACE OF THE VIDEO

If you're the key selling factor of your business, it makes sense for your face to be on the video. To go even further, operational transparency of your business is a great strategy to drive support. The more you let people in behind the scenes, the more they want to do business with you.

However, it's worth considering the future of your business: if you tie your company's brand and your personal brand together, it'll be much harder to sell your business without you attached to it. But if you create a brand that stands by itself, you'll get a higher valuation when you sell it.

For now, just know that if you put yourself on videos associated with the business, you're now inextricably tying yourself to your company's brand.

And unless you're Brad Pitt, don't expect your face alone to bring in millions of views. You have to provide value first and foremost.

Picture the scene again. You're watching TV at home, and your favorite show is interrupted with a commercial break.

Instead of picking up your phone to scroll through Facebook, you open up YouTube. What do you see there?

You see your own video. You smile, knowing that your video marketing works much better and at a much lower cost than if you'd purchased one of the commercial slots you're currently ignoring on television.

Part 2

Driving Traffic

CHAPTER 8

Google Ads that Create Desire

Why was the Yellow Pages directory so successful for over one hundred years?

Think about their sales pitch. When a prospective buyer picks up the Yellow Pages, they find the businesses that are geographically servicing in their area. It was the perfect way to advertise, because buyers are looking for specific products and services. Not only do they have their wallet in one hand and phone in the other, but they're already convinced that they need what you have to offer.

However, since the inception of Google and other search engines, the printed Yellow Pages has become almost obsolete. Today, prospective buyers use their *phones*—not phone books—to look for services and businesses. However, the premise of search engine advertising now is the same as the premise of the Yellow Pages once was.

When you advertise through Google, you can either market to people who are physically in your area, or you can choose which keywords or phrases trigger your ad.

In the Yellow Pages, the amount your ad was worth was dictated *to* you. You paid for your ad to be a specific size, regardless of how well it performed. As a business, you could only hope for the directory to be distributed to everyone in your area, hope that the customers who needed your service would open your ad, and that your competitors spent less than you did.

The whole process was based on hope, and your ROI was unpredictable. Google Ads are much more predictable.

Unlike the Yellow Pages, it costs nothing to have your ad show up on Google. The cost comes when someone *clicks* on your ad—it's a pay-per-click model. Moreover, when you post a Google Ad campaign, you know you can physically serve the people who click on it, because you predetermine the radius in which you want your ad to appear. Not bad, eh?

So as a business, how do you use Google Ads that create desire in your business?

TYPES OF CAMPAIGNS

Imagine you own a pizza restaurant and choose to advertise pizza online within your radius of free delivery. Google Ads can help target people searching for pizza close to your restaurant, with an offer for free delivery. Alternatively, you might run a separate campaign to a broader geographic area for people who are willing to travel across town to eat at your restaurant.

What's more, you can set up different ad campaigns for different products, too. For example, Action Furnace has locations in two different cities. They have separate campaigns for furnace sales in city one and another in city two, and they also run separate campaigns for furnace repair and air conditioning. Why would you want to run separate campaigns? Each campaign allows you to dedicate budget individually and achieve particular goals.

You have to ask yourself: what matters more to my business—where my customers come from, or what product I have to offer them? The answer to that question will help you decide whether you focus on geography, product, or a little of both with your advertisements.

HOW MUCH TO INVEST

To determine how much to invest in an ad campaign, work backward.

Imagine you're an event planner trying to sell 10,000 tickets to a concert you've organized. In this case, you'll have a target acquisition cost per ticket. For example, say the average ticket costs the attendee $100. If you want a 15 percent marketing cost, you want to spend only $15 getting each butt into each seat. This is your cost per acquisition.

Now, before you actually implement your ad campaign, you need to find out how effective your website is at converting ad clicks to ticket sales. To find this out, look at your Google Analytics (or hire someone to do it for you). Maybe one hundred people click on your ad and twenty buy tickets—that would make your website conversion rate a healthy 20 percent.

> Keep in mind that you'll have a different bid strategy for Google searches compared to digital display campaigns (discussed in chapter 9).

So let's do the math...

The average ticket is $100, and you want to acquire each ticket sale for $15 (a 15 percent marketing cost), and your website converts 20 percent (or 1/5) of clicks into sales. If you divide $15 by 20 percent, you have a $3 target *click* cost. In this case, if you spend $3 acquiring traffic to your website, you will yield a 15 percent marketing cost.

In advertising, bids are everything. If your target cost per acquisition is only $3 and your website converts only 5 percent, your click cost must not exceed 15¢.

Someone looking for a specific concert ticket is further along in the buying cycle than many other prospective customers. This type of customer will convert faster and at a higher percentage than, say, a car buyer.

The point is, the more effective your website, the more you can spend on traffic, because each click on an ad is more likely to convert into a sale.

The next step to successful advertising is choosing keywords that fit your target click cost.

ONE BID AFTER ANOTHER

Google Advertising is an auction. Every time a search query is made, an auction occurs, and one of the deciding factors in where your ad ranks is how much you're willing to bid on a click (the other factor is how well you're running your campaigns).

Not only can you change the geographical area of where your ads are triggered to show up, you can also change how much you bid based on that geography. You might decide you're willing to pay $5 per click if a customer is within a mile of your company, or $4 per click if they're two miles away.

You can also bid according to *device*. For example, you might want to bid more for a prospect on their phone versus one on their desktop, or vice versa.

As you gather more data on which Google Ads work the best, that data will determine whether you increase or decrease your bids. Your analytics will show you which keywords are generating clicks and conversions.

ADVANCED TIPS

Tip 1: In most cases, people bid too low. If you bid too low, you risk your ad showing up in an unfavorable position or not showing up at all. You want to aim for the top position, as this is where people are looking and clicking. And, to be frank, you can win bids for less money than you think anyway.

Tip 2: Google Analytics ties into your Google advertising campaign, and if you aren't already using Google Analytics, I encourage you to do so or find someone who can help you.

COMMON MISTAKES

As we've already discussed, many businesses fail to put enough gas in their advertising tank. If you invest only $500 a month in search engine advertising, you won't see much change in your business. Say the average click cost is $5 in your industry. In an entire month, you'll get one hundred clicks ($500 budget divided by $5 clicks). Divide that by thirty days and you end up with three clicks a day. If your website converts clicks into phone calls at 10 percent, it takes you over three days to get a single phone call. If your phone calls convert customers at a 50 percent rate, it takes six days to convert one customer.

Does earning one customer every six days excite you? That answer probably depends on the value of each customer.

Any advertising you do should be profitable. If you spend $3,000, you want your return to look like $30,000. *That's* when you start seeing a big difference in your bottom line. And you can't get that return without a big investment.

ALL ABOUT THE KEYWORDS

Many businesses rush to create Google Ads themselves without becoming properly educated first. They might bid on ten keywords or fewer because they assume this is the magic number to generate queries for their business. In reality, there are thousands of keyword combinations that can generate sales for your business, no matter what industry you're in, because no two people search the same way.

Imagine someone in the HR staffing industry is choosing

keywords for an ad campaign. That person might assume people are searching Google for:

- Temps
- Temp workers
- Hire staff

While these are all accurate keyword phrases, there are thousands of other phrases people use for different job types. For example, people might search for:

- Operation staff
- Reception staff
- Admin staff for hire
- $15-an-hour-max temping agency

The bottom line is: there are *so many ways* to search for what your business has to offer. Google and other services have online tools that can help you identify search trends to add to your campaigns and give you a starting point for using keywords.

Your limited daily budget will stop you from getting inundated with thousands of calls and spending more money than you can afford. For example, if your total budget is $1,000 a month (broken down to $33 a day), Google will continually show your ad throughout the day until your $33 has been spent. If your average click cost is $5, your ad will continue to show up until you get approximately six clicks.

KNOW YOUR PROFITS

Another common mistake is failing to understand the profitability of the different products and services of your business. Imagine you run a car dealership in your city. Selling a car and repairing a car might have totally different profit centers. You might be willing to spend more to sell a car than to fix one, or vice versa.

Moreover, if you have two (or more) products or services operating under the same roof, bidding the same amount for every keyword is a missed opportunity to maximize your profits. Understand the profit you can make from each of your products and services and adjust your bid amounts to reflect your margins. Higher margin products allow for a more aggressive bid strategy, while lower margin products don't allow enough wiggle room for an aggressive strategy.

In the furnace world, the average price for a duct cleaning might be $350, while the average price for a new furnace is $5,000. Let's say a furnace website converts at 10 percent. It makes no sense to spend $30 per click for a duct cleaning ad, because they'll be paying $300 to acquire a customer who will only spend $350. This is an example of nonprofitable marketing (unless your strategy is to find duct cleaning jobs as a loss leader to earn the customer relationship for the chance at a future furnace sale).

It makes more sense to spend $30 per click if they can sell a *new* furnace. In that case, they might gladly spend $300, because earning $5,000 on those jobs makes investing $300 a very profitable decision.

DON'T SET AND FORGET

The world of advertising is dynamic, not static. Competitors will come and leave. Your customers' search habits will change. New technology will be developed, and better practices will be established.

If you hire a junior salesperson to join your company, you can expect to spend time training and working with them. Treat a campaign the same way. Any successful advertising campaign requires constant effort and optimization. To set a campaign and forget about it presents a huge missed opportunity.

PLAYING WITH MONEY

To launch an ad campaign, start with a budget that you can afford to lose. Consider it research and development. While you might expect some return, finance your first thirty to sixty days in a way that won't bankrupt you or cause fights at the dinner table.

Then, set up conversion tracking so you can calculate the profit you're generating with your Google Ads.

If you don't know how to set up these processes, hire an agency or consultant to come in and do it for you, because the setup is important. For a campaign to generate money, you need to have the right reporting in place. This is a crucial opportunity for you to exponentially grow your business.

When your campaign is set up correctly and your ads reach people interested in your products and services, you'll yield a profitable result.

BUILD THE FORMULA

No matter how much research and development you're doing on your Google Ads, do *not* blow through your entire marketing budget in the first thirty days of a campaign. Instead, focus on building the formula. One company's website conversion rate might be 2 percent while another's is 18 percent. These rates will drastically change how you should bid.

Take the first thirty to sixty days as a tester. When you get the numbers back, reread this chapter. Think about your bidding strategies. Calculate your website conversion rates. You might find you need a better website, better messaging, better content, or a better strategy altogether.

THE MOST EFFECTIVE FORM OF MARKETING

Google Ads still stands as the single most effective form of marketing I've seen throughout my entire digital marketing career. Through search engine advertising, you're only spending money on the people you can serve. You can determine how much you're willing to pay for someone to click on your ad.

> While Google has the highest percentage of market share, other search engines like Bing and Yahoo! operate in similar ways and can host effective advertising campaigns as well.

When you pay for an ad to appear in the Yellow Pages, you're stuck with it for a year. With search engine advertising, you have the chance to make more immediate changes. If an ad is working, you can continue to invest more in the campaign. If an ad isn't working, you can pause it immediately. As a business, you have the capability to reach more or fewer people whenever you want.

Search engine advertising simultaneously takes all the benefits of the Yellow Pages and removes all of its negatives. If you're wondering why Google Ads operates in the billions of dollars per quarter, it's because they created a product for business owners unlike anything else on the market.

CHAPTER 9

Digital Display Campaigns

Imagine you're reading an article on CNN about the state of the economy in your region. Suddenly, a banner ad fills up part of your screen. It's *your business's* banner ad, helping to create awareness of your company to an audience of people who live within your city. Most people assume that these banners are only bought by big companies. Nike. Apple. Pizza Hut.

In reality, there's no reason banners can't work for a local business like yours, too. Local business ads could actually work *more* effectively, because your information is more relevant for the people browsing in your city.

Let's use the pizza restaurant example again. Mondays are your slowest night of the week, so you create a two-for-one offer that is only available on Mondays. Traditionally, you might spread the word through direct mail. You might hang a sign on a street corner or place an ad in a local newspaper. If you're really adventurous, you might create a radio ad to play on Mondays.

But with digital display campaigns, you can spread the word about your two-for-one offer *online*. You could geographically target your delivery area. You could run the ad on Monday nights from 4:00 p.m. to 10:00 p.m. (from open to close). You could target eighteen- to forty-year-olds, as this might be your main target demographic for this particular promotion.

Digital display campaigns have all the benefits of traditional advertising but focus on the right customer at the right time, without having to show up on Google search (like Google Ads).

OPTIMIZING CAMPAIGNS

There are various ways to pay for digital display campaigns. For example, you could pay every time an ad shows up or every time someone clicks. Alternatively, you could pay every time a customer converts. As a business owner and marketer, you can choose how and when you wish to pay. The advertising platform is still an auction, so the more you're willing to pay, the more likely you'll show up in prominent positions on websites.

You can also determine how much each action is worth. For example, you might want to pay $10 every time your ad is shown 1,000 times or 50¢ whenever someone clicks on your ad.

WORTH THE RISK?

While paying per acquisition (or conversion) is the least risky method, it will cost you the most. Paying for an impression is the least expensive, because you don't know if a customer will click or purchase. The amazing benefit of digital display advertising is the ability to pay more for prospects who are further down the buying funnel. The more likely they are to buy your product *today* reflects where your prospect sits in the buying funnel. If your prospect's online behavior reflects that they are simply researching how your product works, they aren't as close to buying your product as they are if they are researching shipping methods or your return policy.

The beauty of marketing is that it gives you the freedom to try. This month, you can try one bidding strategy. Next month, you can try another. The month after that, you can try a third. Play around and see which strategy works best for you.

You can change your messaging whenever you want. For example, you might have one offer on Mondays and a totally different offer on Tuesdays or Wednesdays. You could even have one offer for Monday morning and a different one for Monday afternoon.

Remember, your ads can say whatever you want them to say. You could have unlimited campaigns running at one time; the time and geographic parameters are totally up to you.

DESIGN

If your company has an internal graphic design resource, you can design your ads internally. If not, I recommend hiring a graphic designer. Local students are a great place to start, or you could find freelancers through websites like Fiverr.com.

RETARGETING

You can advertise to new prospects through digital display. You can also advertise to prospects who know about you through retargeting. The idea behind retargeting is simple: provide specific advertising and messaging to a particular group of people based on how they behave on your website. Here's what I mean: your customer visits a particular product page on your website, or they come to you from your email marketing, or they bought an item directly on your website—depending on what action they took, you can bucket them into a particular audience group and then show them specific ads and messages.

The first time I ever experienced this was in my early twenties. I'd just moved out of my own place and moved into a condo with my future wife. For the first time in my life, I had some disposable income, and as a twenty-three-year-old kid dreading the prospect of keeping a condo neat, I wanted the best (laziest), most twenty-three-year-old purchase I could think of: I wanted to buy a robotic vacuum.

But before I made the purchase, I did some research. The one I wanted cost $600. I put it in my online shopping cart thinking I might want to buy it, but once I checked with my girlfriend (now wife), she enlightened me that $600 for a vacuum was too much at the time.

So I left that little shopping cart icon in the top-right corner sitting with the "1" in the image, representing that lonely little robotic vacuum I had yet to purchase and walked away without purchasing.

After I left that site, the retailer retargeted me. They knew I was close to making the purchase, but I just hadn't pulled the trigger. They knew there was no better prospect to target than someone who was seconds away from buying their product.

So, all the sudden, I start seeing ads about the robotic vacuum everywhere. I see ads when I'm checking my email, looking up the weather, and watching sports highlights. They email me a $50-off coupon, then they include free shipping. Finally, ads with product benefit statements start popping up every time I turned on my computer. In the end, the final cost of that vacuum fell far lower than the $600 price tag I originally came across.

In the end, with such a small condo, I couldn't justify (to my wife) actually spending hundreds of dollars to save a few minutes each week in vacuuming. But let's say I *did* decide to click buy, and it's in the mail.

The company would now know that I'm their ideal shopper: they had retargeted me, and it had worked. Knowing that, the company could begin to retarget me even more. It's now thirty days later, and they want to sell me their next invention: the Robo-Mop! I would only be seeing these ads now because of my propensity and likelihood to buy their products. This strategy can be extremely effective, as marketing dollars are being invested to target ideal customers who have a history of buying from you.

So, essentially, retargeting is another marketing strategy based on what we know about the people who have been to our website.

To create your own retargeting campaign, map out the customer journey and ask yourself some questions:

Who are my customers?

What are they buying?

When are they buying?

What are complementary products?

What are the obstacles to buying?

When they come to my website and they don't buy, why not?

What other advertising can I put in front of them? And when?

Alert: You need enough people coming to your website to develop this audience list. If you have a small number of website visits, then you have nobody to retarget. Ensure this strategy is layered onto other digital marketing efforts that generate a ton of qualified traffic.

Based on your answers to those questions, you *can* build complex and robust marketing strategies for retargeting. However, in order to develop audience lists, you need enough people to visit your website. If you have a small website with few visitors, you don't have an audience for retargeting. On the other hand, Amazon can retarget to a million people in an hour.

The success of your retargeting strategy depends on

traffic. The more people who visit your site, the more opportunities you have to retarget to people. Find ways to reach people through display advertising and search engine optimization.

ASK AROUND

Keep in mind that the costs associated with a traditional advertiser are much higher than if you go through an agency or advertise yourself. The digital package available from your local newspaper or radio station is probably priced between $10 and $15 per thousand impressions.

If you advertise yourself or go through an agency, you might be able to buy the same quantity of impressions for half the cost. The benefit of buying through a radio or television company is the bundle they can offer with traditional media and a high-frequency audience. The appeal of investing with one company and being on many platforms is strong, and these conglomerates are also investing their resources to develop new technologies and ways to reach even more prospects.

I recommend asking around. Get quotes. Not all digital is sold equal, so it's a good idea to ask how people are charging.

For example, local city newspapers sell banner ads (as part of a package) at $12 per thousand impressions. However, when they have leftover inventory, many of them sell this inventory to Google or other display networks, which allows advertisers to purchase the same ad space at a fraction of the cost.

CREATING CAMPAIGNS

When creating your display campaigns for your business, think about all of the products, services, and brands that you offer. How many of these could be their own campaign? When designing a campaign, you'll want to showcase the product (service or brand) with a strong image. You can either add a specific offer to that product or include a call to action. Remember, always think about what you want the prospect to do next.

Another strategy to implement is to target your campaigns to the specific desired audiences you are looking to attract to your business. For example, if you own a traditional furniture retail store, your image should include a popular couch that you sell with an offer, such as "25% Off Sofas and Loveseats This Weekend Only!" The target of this campaign should be to people who are most likely to buy that particular couch. Are they an older demographic? Male? Female? In comparison, Wayfair targets people with a similar advertisement, but to people who are most likely to buy furniture online. You can find and target to these audience lists for each of your campaigns.

CHAPTER 10

Social Media

To be clear, I am not a social media publisher myself. I have never directly run social media platforms for any client (or even for my own business). What I offer instead of direct experience is a particular outlook—I'm a business owner and entrepreneur—just like you. I understand the potential of social media for small business. However, I find myself lacking the time available to execute it *myself*. My time is needed elsewhere in my business.

Don't get me wrong, social media offers incredible opportunities for both your business and mine. Authors like Gary Vaynerchuk and Seth Godin have written amazing books about what social media has done for their respective businesses. While they're not wrong, social media requires commitment. Unless you're committed to doing it right, social media will be a waste of your time.

DO IT RIGHT

I am going to do you a favor:

I give you permission to *never* do social media again.

I have seen businesses grow exponentially without Facebook, Instagram, or any other social media platforms. My most successful client, Action Furnace, has grown exponentially over the last five years with *zero* social media strategy. They haven't posted a single organic Facebook or Instagram post in their existence, and instead they've chosen to invest heavily on advertising instead.

The point is, you have to put that effort somewhere. It doesn't have to be in social media—it can be in other content creation or digital advertising—but if you choose to use it, here's how to go about it.

If you aren't spending time strategizing on your social media and instead just uploading quick posts because you feel the pressure to pump out content, you're not only wasting your time, you're wasting your audience's time, too.

However, if you put together a strategic plan to create content that people actually care about and distribute it on various channels, social media can be an extremely effective form of digital marketing.

Most entrepreneurs haven't mastered social media. If you're committed to social media as a tool, either become *the* expert in your business yourself or hire an expert or an agency to do the job for you. That way, you have a guarantee that it'll be done well.

Think of social media as a conversation with your audience as they sit in that lull between sales and transactions. For example, social media is a great tool for increasing awareness about your products and services. However, keep in mind that the majority of people who choose to follow you will either already be customers or heavily intend to become customers already.

TELL YOUR STORY WELL

Even if social media isn't bringing in new customers to your business, it is still a great tool to build loyalty, culture, and brand perception. It's so effective because it is a powerful platform to tell your story. If you truly believe in the power of social media, invest the time and resources to craft your story properly.

Through social media, you can share your story in the following ways:

- Show your customers the people behind your business (employees, etc.).
- Educate customers on your products and services and the benefits they provide.

- Create a positive emotional connection between your company and your audience.

Tentree is a Canadian clothing apparel company. One of their social media strategies is to plant ten trees for every item of clothing a customer buys. Giving back to the environment is a great cause that has helped launch their business.

I learned about the strategy by way of a video they posted on Facebook. The video announced a collaboration between tentree and the Canadian Wildlife Federation. The campaign was designed to show the lifestyle of the people who wear the brand's clothing. Watching their aspirational video helped me identify with their brand. On top of that, I knew that buying a T-shirt would also lead to ten new trees being planted. Naturally, I went on their website and bought from them.

These are some of the ideas behind tentree's social media posts:

What do we need to save the boreal forest?

Learn about what we plant in Madagascar.

These five cities plant the most trees:

Plant more trees. Young forests use carbon most effectively.

Interestingly, their social media features very little about their clothing. There are hardly any models wearing shirts, hats, belts, or pants, as you would expect from a clothing company.

Instead, tentree's social media pages are exclusively dedicated to their cause and story. Their strategy is based around planting ten trees at a time, which is what the company does. They just happen to sell shirts as well.

As a potential customer scrolling through tentree's social media, I get a positive impression about the brand and its cause. Then, when I do want to buy someone a gift or buy myself another shirt, I am inclined to purchase from tentree. I know that wearing their logo represents their story.

When we visit social media, we want to be entertained. Nobody visits social media to buy or be intentionally influenced. We scroll to catch up with friends, family members, and companies we care about. Tentree is educating their social media followers about issues they care about. If you're a tentree customer, you probably care about the environment and the company's cause. The more they share on social media, the more positive you feel about the company overall. This strategy increases customer loyalty and trust, much more than if they just told you to buy their shirts.

YOU'VE ALREADY HIRED A MASTER

As a business owner, if you don't go down the social media rabbit hole, you don't have to master it yourself. Recognize that there are probably people in your organization who are *already* better suited to carry out the next steps than you are. Find these people and put them to good use. In our agency, we have built an internal team who has helped us form our social media strategy and execution. Before them, it was a shared responsibility between several people in the organization (content curators, publishers, etc.).

Once you identify that in-house expert, determine your strategy. Decide what you want social media to accomplish for you. Write the brand guidelines. For example, you might vow to never respond publicly or make anyone feel bad about themselves.

As a brand, what values do you stand behind?

Think about a publication schedule. Write out nine categories of content that you could produce. Nine categories of content is a good number to focus on with Instagram, as your "grid" displays rows of photos in sets of three.

Having nine categories maintains a consistent strategy while providing some diversity in appearance. On Instagram, you can share videos and photos only. On Facebook, you can share articles as well.

Some categories include:

- inspirational quotes
- men's lifestyle
- family-focused
- food and cuisine
- product shots
- employee profiles

For each category, define the parameters of your content. For example, you might decide to only upload inspirational quotes from business leaders or philanthropists who share the same values as your company.

Next, assign the content curation, whether to your team or another company. Their job is to find content, pictures, stories, images, and articles to fit into your categories. I recommend using a shared drive system (Google Drive, Dropbox, or shared office desktop) to create folders. Create a folder for each category. The person in charge of curating the content finds it and drops it into these folders.

Remember: You don't have to create 100 percent custom content, especially if you're a small or medium-sized business. You're allowed to buy stock images, download articles, and find videos on YouTube. There are countless ways to find content, as long as you give appropriate credit to the person who originally posted it.

Finally, the decision-maker (you or someone you assign) approves or rejects the content in the folders. Once content is approved, it can be scheduled out according to the publication order. You can preschedule content or your staff can manually post with whatever frequency works for you. Hootsuite is one example of a scheduling software, but countless other programs exist, too.

Follow these steps with intention, and you'll have a dialed-in social media strategy before you know it.

A CONVERSATION

When you break social media down into digestible parts, it doesn't feel as overwhelming. Plan the type of content you need to create, decide where you're going to find it, and assign people to curate it for you. That's how you create a consistent and meaningful conversation between you and your customers on social media.

Think of social media as a two-way street. When committing to social media, you're committing to a conversation. Not only should you post information people care about, but just as we discussed in chapter 4 in reference to complaints and reviews, you should always respond to comments and questions that customers leave for you online. Follow other brands you respect and leave comments on their posts.

> Social media isn't merely a platform to announce to the world who you are. Social media is about providing value. In his book *Jab, Jab, Jab, Right Hook,* Gary Vaynerchuk preaches the idea of "giving" through social media. Give, give, give. Give content. Give advice. Give value. That way, when you ask for something in return, people are more likely to respond.

I'm not asking you to master social media overnight. I'm asking you to first decide how you want social media to work for you and your company. If you want to commit to social media, find people who are creative and can tell your story properly.

If you don't want to commit to social media, then stay away from it altogether. Either way is valid, as long as you're doing what's best for you and your company, based on the time and resources you have and the objectives you set out.

Part 3

Measuring

CHAPTER 11

Measuring ROI

An old adage claims that only half of marketing is effective...and the business owner usually doesn't know which half.

As discussed throughout this book, digital marketing has the ability to peek behind the numbers and see what's working and what's not. With digital marketing, you can understand the impact of every piece of advertising and content you put into the world. You can track how many times somebody sees an ad, you can see what someone did before and after seeing your ad, and you can track what pages they visited on your website and how long they spent on each page.

When a customer is online and engaged with your digital marketing, *all* information is available to you.

That information can help you identify which forms of marketing are effective and which are ineffective. You can determine which marketing is too expensive and the types of ads you need more of. So how do you measure your ROI when it comes to digital marketing?

It starts with conversions.

WHAT IS A CONVERSION?

Before you can track conversions, you need to identify what a conversion is. This will be different for every business.

For example, if you're a small-medium business that deals with offline sales and in-person interactions, a conversion will either be a phone call to your business, an email or form fill, or someone walking into your retail location.

For a company selling goods online, a conversion might be a prospective customer signing up to your email newsletter, downloading a white paper, calling to inquire about your services, or making a purchase directly from your website.

Whatever your conversion looks like, you have to identify what it is before you can move to the next step.

NEXT STEPS

After you determine your conversion, get started with Google Analytics. In Google Analytics, you can set up conversions as a goal or event (these are when people on your website take an action that you wanted them to). That way, whenever a conversion happens on your website, Google Analytics can track it.

Naturally, an offline conversion is more difficult to track. Companies are already working on ways to fix that, and businesses with physical locations will be able to correlate walk-in traffic to their digital marketing efforts. If a customer walks into your store with a cell phone, Google may be able to tell whether that cell phone user has searched your business website within a particular time period. Pretty wild, huh? It's coming, and you want to be on the forefront of those developments.

Once you discern where your conversions are coming from, you can calculate whether the cost of an advertising medium is worth the number of conversions. This is the cost per conversion for an advertising attribution.

For example, say you spend $1,000 on a Facebook campaign and get fifty conversions. The cost per conversion for your Facebook campaign is $20.

It's a good idea to compare different costs for conversions

across the board. Look at Facebook conversions compared to email newsletters. When you compare the costs of these conversions, you can make changes to your marketing. If you get a $20 cost per conversion on Facebook and a $30 cost per conversion on Instagram, it makes sense to reallocate money back into Facebook advertising because it's more profitable.

E-COMMERCE

If you run an e-commerce business, chances are that you already have these processes in place. And if you don't, you have no excuse. The beauty of e-commerce is that you know how much you sell and the value of each transaction. You can track the conversion of an e-commerce business easily by entering exact revenue dollars and the ROI.

PHONE CALLS

My guess is that you want to know how to track phone call conversions. Two examples of tracking software are CallRail and ActiveDEMAND. When a prospective customer visits your website, this software replaces your phone number with a call tracking number. That way, when a customer calls you, the tracking number reroutes the call back to you while simultaneously intercepting the information of the call. As a result, you learn what brought the caller to your website, what page was opened, and what their digital journey was prior to making that phone call.

Call tracking software can also provide call recording. As a marketer or business owner, you can audit the quality of the phone call to determine if you want to follow the transaction one step further. If you correlate the caller information with your customer CRM, you can determine ROI.

Imagine three prospects do a search for your product category and come across your website. One calls you and talks to a member of your sales staff. At the end of the month, you can listen to that phone call and come to conclusions about the validity of this prospect and the quality of your sales staff to close the deals.

For example, I can go into our CRM and see if that prospect signs up as a new customer. Not only that, but I can see how much they spent. Let's say they spent $1,000. I attribute that to my Facebook campaign, because I conclude that a Facebook ad brought the decision-maker to my website.

TRACKING YOUR PROGRESS

The purpose of this book is to help you create a plan. The first step is to make a plan. The second step is to launch it with the right budget. The third is to understand what works and what doesn't.

Failing to track your marketing effectiveness is the same

as having a team of salespeople selling your products and not understanding who sold what. How do you know who needs more training, coaching, or management? Just like you track sales, you should track marketing. With automated software like ActiveDEMAND or HubSpot, you have no excuse not to keep track of every aspect of your conversions.

Initially, having access to all this data might feel overwhelming. Don't panic.

You can build automated reports that clearly show your cost per lead. For example, a report will tell you how many opportunities you generated, how much you spent, and your cost per lead for a specific medium. If you reconcile every month or every quarter, this information will be extremely useful. Investing a few hours to pull together this information could save you from investing too much money in a bad marketing campaign.

Say you have five campaigns on Facebook. You could have a campaign for each product you sell or city you service. For each campaign, you can determine your cost per lead/cost per acquisition for a specific service, product, or geography. Once you have this information, you can decide whether you want to continue a campaign, change the messaging, or end it altogether.

In our agency, we do all the measurements for clients and are able to effectively measure their ROI. When you work with a strong agency, you can be confident that their recommendations are properly informed.

MAKING CHANGES

Once you determine your target cost per acquisition, you can work backward to figure out a target cost per lead or opportunity.

At Action Furnace, our target *lead* is $100. If we can make the phone ring for under $100, we know it's a profitable lead. We use this baseline of $100 as an acceptable metric to evaluate what marketing works and what doesn't. We're happy to reinvest into any solution producing leads that cost less than $100. If we see anything above, we make a decision on whether to adjust the campaign or cancel it.

Understandably, some business owners have a hard time letting go of certain strategies. For example, many old-school businesses rely almost exclusively on newspaper advertising to generate customers. With the rise of online publications, more and more newspapers are going out of business. As such, their effectiveness is decreasing dramatically. If you were to look at the cost per lead on a newspaper ad now, you probably wouldn't want to invest in it.

And yet people still do. I continually see businesses invest in newspaper advertising because they have a great relationship with their sales rep, for example. Ask yourself if that relationship is worth the investment you're making in it, because that advertising avenue is not going to last for long, and the ROI you're generating for your business is not as high as it could be.

> Just because a strategy has worked in the past, that doesn't mean it'll continue to work forever.

CHANGE IS GOOD

We worked with one of the top three residential home builders in our city. Because they built their entire business through newspaper advertising, they were incredibly reluctant to let it go. Since working with us, they have a digital budget and can easily see ROI. But they continue to invest in print advertising. Why? The business owner is a great networker who has built a solid relationship with that company and their sales reps.

In my opinion, the company continues to have nonoptimal marketing investments by not letting go of print advertising. Many businesses don't make the switch soon enough. They continue doing what they're doing and then wonder why their business has less revenue, perhaps blaming the economy, millennials, and everything else under the sun.

In reality, consumer behaviors are changing. Customers are changing the way they shop. As a business, you must adapt and adjust to these changes. Change isn't a bad thing. Every business should be changing to keep up with the times. Decreases in revenue might be caused by a lack of willingness to change.

Just give it a try. Dig in and measure your ROI, or you might as well be throwing flyers into the street and hoping for the best.

CHAPTER 12

Do It Yourself or Hire an Agency?

I wish I could give you a simple answer to this question, but there isn't one.

To make the decision, you need to understand your own business.

Where do you want to go?

How aggressive is your growth?

What opportunity do you have ahead?

How much free cash do you have available?

Would your cash flow allow you to hire somebody?

Evaluate your own expertise as an entrepreneur. Then evaluate the expertise of your staff.

Make a list of what you need to be successful. When you have this written out, you can evaluate whether or not you have the expertise in-house. If you don't, you can start looking at the cost of hiring an agency and delegating certain aspects of your marketing out to other people.

WHEN TO HIRE AN AGENCY

As a business owner, you need to decide how much marketing matters to the success of your business.

If you believe that marketing can be your competitive advantage, you should consider hiring an agency or using a consultant (or both). To win the marketing game, you need an expert to come up with your messaging, highlight your competitive advantage, and demonstrate the benefits of working with you.

For some businesses, an agency will do everything you need it to do. For others, it makes more sense to hire someone internally, so that person can coordinate with different departments or different agencies. Maybe that person needs to be at trade shows or helping plan events.

In our company, well, we are an agency, and we *still* have someone dedicated to only marketing our business.

While an agency typically comes with high-level strategy and execution, the internal marketing manager, coordinator, or director decides the marketing strategies for the company.

If you're making over $1 million in revenue, I recommend looking for a fully outsourced agency or utilizing the services of a part-time or full-time marketing person. It's at this milestone in the business that we consistently witness the entrepreneur's capacity for available time shrink while free cash flow increases (enough to pay for outsourced marketing solutions). It's important to be comfortable with any agency you hire. Make sure they understand your business and industry. Look for people you *want* to work with and alongside. Ideally, their domain expertise should match up with what you need, and the passion they exhibit for your business should be second to none.

INTERNAL HIRES: THE STRUGGLE IS REAL

Everybody wants a unicorn. So do I. Sadly for us all, they simply don't exist. The unicorn is someone who is as great at creating strategy as they are developing a website, as creative at graphically designing ads as they are at social media posts, and as masterful with words to create an amazing blog as they are at writing a corporate press release.

Marketing is one of the most diverse segments of business. It encompasses everything from marketing research to international marketing to digital marketing. Even within the world of digital marketing there are different experts. Some are masters of Google advertising and others know YouTube like the back of their hand.

Because marketing is so diverse, there is no one person who is good at everything. Chances are that you'll hire someone who is pretty good at a lot of things but a master of none. If you want quality work, you'll need to outsource it. Even if you hire someone to help with digital advertising, you still need someone to build your website, craft your social media, design your graphic projects, and write all of your content.

TAKE THIS OPPORTUNITY

Your business might be very successful without any advertising. Even if this is the case, I think you'd be missing an opportunity by not engaging in digital marketing.

For some businesses, digital marketing is necessary. If your customers are searching and buying online, you need to market yourself online. The goal is to brand your business to get the right customer.

Effective digital marketing will increase your market share and make it harder for your competitors to sell. Through your marketing, you inform your current customers about new products and services. If this is done well, you increase the average value of your customer and how much they spend with you.

If you aren't investing in digital marketing and advertising, you're missing a huge opportunity to be more successful.

GET THE MOST OUT OF YOUR MARKETING TEAM

When working with marketing professionals, share your definition of success. Clearly define where you want to go. Decide your objectives. Lay out the rules of the game. What does success look like to you? And then share it—with everyone expected to have an impact on achieving the results.

Once you've shared your goals, invest the budget necessary to make success happen. Be open to budget recommendations. Ask questions. If you don't understand someone's thought process, ask them to explain it more clearly.

Stay engaged consistently. When a client is quiet, it's difficult for an agency to be successful because they have no feedback about what's happening in the business. For example, an agency might see a lot of leads coming in but may not be informed that a temp is filling in for the front-of-house person responsible for closing your leads. These details help. Marketing is a big part of your business, so it's crucial to stay engaged with your internal marketer or agency.

> Be patient. Very few salespeople are instantly amazing. The same goes for digital marketers. Marketers have to learn how customers are looking for you and what's causing them to click on ads. It takes time to collect this data and implement changes. Give them time.

DESPERATION GETS YOU NOWHERE

Desperate clients are bad clients because desperation equals poor decision making.

Let me tell you about one client who hired us prematurely. A Californian optometrist who was really ambitious but wasn't actually ready for an agency, nor did he have the cash threshold to support one. He expected our service to be the magic bean that would grow into a beanstalk overnight. Because of his desperation, he convinced us to expedite our process. So we did. We moved a twelve-week project into five weeks.

We worked twice as hard to launch a marketing campaign twice as fast. As soon as the ads went live (I mean within minutes), he was asking where his new patients were.

The sales cycle of any business doesn't last one day, especially if that business is in a position to hire an agency. If you're considering upgrading your mattress, it could be years before you actually pull the trigger. Similarly, an auto body mechanic must wait until someone's car breaks down.

As a business, you can be marketing to people, but those people will only call you when they need your services.

In my business, we depend on time and circumstance. People can hear about us and what we offer, but until they've felt pain or finally realize the opportunity ahead of them, they won't make a change in their marketing.

The problem with the desperate client from my story is that he expected everything to happen overnight. If you hire a salesperson, you can't expect them to meet their *first-year* quota in the first *week*. It's just not going to happen.

Hiring a marketing company is an investment. When you invest in marketing, you need a long-term approach.

You need to understand how your budget is divvied out. Some of that will go toward direct advertising, like Google Ads. This advertising should yield a quicker ROI. The rest of your budget is for branding and building trust with your audience, through the tactics we've discussed like social media, content creation, and video production (among others). That way, when someone needs your product or service in the future, they'll remember you.

Desperation never goes well. Disengagement never goes well. A lack of communication never goes well.

But patience, investment, and care *almost always* yield a healthy ROI.

FLY HIGH

Think of your marketing program as the plane moving toward your ultimate destination. Your flight path is the plan ahead. With that flight path, you know where you're going and what moves you need to make.

Sometimes, customers get on a plane without telling the pilot where they want to go. Misalignment at the beginning of a flight can totally change the flight path. If a plane falls off course just a few degrees on a four-hour flight, it could very well end up on a different continent.

Aim for alignment. Even when you have alignment, read-just it.

Any flight crew constantly checks with ground control to make sure they're on the right path. They're readjusting their path to hit the runway and be on time. If the pilot were simply left alone, how could you expect them to find their destination or know when to land?

Communicate with your digital marketer consistently, so you both get to your destination together.

ONE BIG SALES CYCLE

My best customers understand that marketing is part of a sales cycle. It doesn't happen overnight. Your agency or marketing person should be held to metrics that are within their control.

Remember that marketing brings opportunity to your business, while sales and operations take that opportunity home.

Say our agency generates fifty-eight opportunities for a plumbing company. They only close twelve because they charge a call-out fee (a fee to just come and provide you with a price for the *real* work). Their competitors, however, were waiving this same fee.

Instead of evaluating your marketing based on the twelve (out of fifty-eight) closed deals, marketing should be evaluated based on the fifty-eight opportunities.

What an ad says (ad copy), the bid strategies of the campaigns, and the website experience are all within a marketer's control. As soon as a customer calls a company, that experience is all on that business.

Conclusion

A BLEND OF ART AND SCIENCE

Digital marketing is an art and a science at the same time. The scientific side is the data analytics. The artistic challenge is to make your brand and message look more appealing than the other options in your industry.

Most business owners know they have to improve their marketing, but their excuse is that they never get around to it. Take my advice and block off half a day this week and then every quarter after that. Turn on your *out of office* autoresponder, unplug your phone and any other distractions, and pull in a team of people and discuss your marketing goals, strategic objectives, and definition of success—and create a plan of attack.

In your quarterly reviews, look at how many new customers you serviced. How much did you spend to acquire them? According to your reporting, are you on track with your marketing plan? Did you reach all of your quarterly objectives? How much revenue did you earn? Are you seeing the right type of customer? How effective is your marketing compared to your sales? These questions are all important to review on a consistent basis.

This book only scratches the surface of digital marketing. Everything else you want to learn can be found online, in other books, or on blogs. But you have to go out and learn it.

If you aren't willing to learn, then it's time to call on experts who can help you.

Try things. No science or art is complete without experimentation. Because marketing trends (as well as consumers) change so often, you have to have money and time set aside for research and development.

The digital marketing landscape is changing for the better. Are you going to change with it?

Acknowledgments

This page is a really important one for me, as I believe that publishing a book requires a team, a community. Whether the impact was felt directly within the pages of this book or through other experiences that impacted the words on the page, everyone below has played a role in the creation of this book.

To begin, I'd like to focus on my family. The first person I'd like to thank is my beautiful wife, Lea. Your fierce support of these crazy projects, my career, and overall ambitions is remarkable. Your sacrifices are not lost on me, and I'm forever grateful for having you in my life. To my children, Carter, Aviana, and Mateo, your unconditional love and admiration are my fuel each and every day. I apologize you're not mentioned in this book other than this page, but as I explained over countless dinners, this is a book about growing your business and having children is a business with no sight of a return on investment. I love you all!

To my mom and dad, thank you both for telling me I could literally do anything I wanted and be anything I wanted to in life. You equipped me with the confidence to start a book and the work ethic to finish it. To my sister, Amanda, not only are you the bomb sister, but you've chosen your career to work alongside me and support my dreams. For that, I appreciate you and thank you for giving it everything you have.

Next, I'd like to thank my work family. Bruce, thank you for giving me the confidence to step out of my comfort zone and start our agency. Your outlook and mentorship continues to shape me each and every day. Also, thank you for allowing me to use you *throughout* this book. You are a true business inspiration. To Karim, thank you for your relentless support of me and our companies. I'm glad we're on this ride together. To Trudi, thank you for pushing me into areas of business and the globe I never would have gotten to on my own. Your drive and tenacity are second to none and push me every day. To Wade and Jason, you guys are rock stars and make my life easy. Thank you for having my back and taking on every challenge I throw your way.

To my entire team who I am lucky enough to go into

battle with every day: thank you for everything you do and who you are. I am blessed to have the privilege to go into the office and collaborate and learn from each and every one of you. Thank you for teaching me many of the main points in this book. It wouldn't have been written without your hard work.

To my EO (Entrepreneurs Organization) Forum: Jason, Brian, Addison, Kyle, Matt, Quinn, and Andrew. There is no better forum across the globe than ours and I am truly grateful that you asked me to join. The support, guidance, and friendship I receive from you has helped bring this book to life. We were together at our forum retreat in Salt Lake City when we saw Tucker Max on stage explaining why someone would ever want to write a book. From there, I knew I would, but your support of the idea has been amazing.

I would also like to thank my entire EO Chapter in Calgary as the organization continues to be a beacon of support, providing exceptional learning events, amazing speakers, and once-in-a-lifetime opportunities.

Last, I would like to thank my team at Scribe for their contributions. They made this process much less difficult than it would have been without them. Their entire process for supporting entrepreneurs to bring to life a book is well thought out and intentionally effective. Thank you to Bailey, Greg, Seth, and Cindy for all that you did.

A special thank you to both Cameron Martel and Andrew Obrecht for your contributions in helping me come up with the name for my book. Naming stuff can be really tough, and you made it easier for me.

About the Author

KEVIN WILHELM has seen the evolution of digital marketing firsthand since 2008. He started his marketing career working for the largest media agency in Canada (Yellow Pages), assisting the transformation from print to online before becoming the director of marketing for the largest childcare provider in Canada, BrightPath Early Learning. Kevin now serves as the president of POD Marketing, a network of marketing agencies he co-founded in 2014. What started with one client has grown to more than one hundred, from one employee to over thirty, and from the struggles of bootstrapping a startup to generating millions in recurring revenue.

CPSIA information can be obtained
at www.ICGtesting.com
Printed in the USA
LVHW030209100919
630502LV00005B/6